Kári Gíslason was born in Reykjavík in 1972. He moved to England at the age of ten, and then to Australia four years later. He was awarded a doctorate in 2003 for his thesis on medieval Icelandic literature and also writes scholarly articles, travel journalism, and reviews. Kári is Associate Professor of Creative Writing at Queensland University of Technology. In 2015 he published his second book, the novel *The Ash Burner*, and he is co-author with Richard Fidler of *Saga Land: The Island of Stories at the Edge of the World* (2017).

PRAISE FOR *THE PROMISE OF ICELAND*

'A deeply charming account of displacement, of not really knowing where you come from and how that makes it difficult to know where you belong.' *Sunday Mail* 'Book of the Week'

'An honest, contemplative and heartfelt journey across generations, landscapes and . . . the truth and mythology of family.' *Weekend Gold Coast Bulletin*

'A powerful memoir about landscape and identity.' *Adelaide Advertiser*

'What Gíslason does particularly well is ʳ
signi ficance of place in people's liv

Also by Kári Gíslason

The Ash Burner
Saga Land (with Richard Fidler)

THE PROMISE
OF ICELAND

Kári Gíslason

The two verses of the Old Norse poem, 'Sonatorrek', on page 138 are quoted from the 1976 Penguin Classics translation of *Egil's Saga* by Hermann Pálsson and Paul Edwards. The lullaby, 'Sofðu unga ástin mín', that appears on pages 264 and 265 is by the Icelandic poet and playwright Jóhann Sigurjónsson (1880–1919). For various reasons, the author has changed the names of some people in this memoir but has been faithful to the truth in his narrative.

First published 2011 by University of Queensland Press
PO Box 6042, St Lucia, Queensland 4067 Australia
Reprinted 2015, 2016, 2017, 2021

www.uqp.com.au
reception@uqp.com.au

Cataloguing-in-Publication entry is available from
the National Library of Australia
http://catalogue.nla.gov.au/

978 0 7022 3906 9 (pbk)
978 0 7022 4680 7 (epub)
978 0 7022 4681 4 (kindle)
978 0 7022 4679 1 (pdf)

Cover design by gogoGingko
Front cover photograph by katyjones.tv
Back cover photograph from author's private collection
Typeset in 11/15 pt Minion by Post Pre-press Group, Brisbane
Printed in Australia by McPherson's Printing Group

University of Queensland Press uses papers that are natural, renewable and recyclable products made from wood grown in well-managed forests and other controlled sources. The logging and manufacturing processes conform to the environmental regulations of the country of origin.

For my mother

CONTENTS

My mother liked to joke that he was the only nervous adulterer in Iceland, and that it said a lot about her that she'd managed to be with him. All these years after their affair ended he was still frightened by it, and with so much going on in his mind he couldn't see his way clear to talk about us as father and son. Had he managed to, I might have told him that I was thinking about living in Iceland, and then we might have met half-way.

I had first contacted him at work, struggling on the phone with my childlike Icelandic to explain who I was. I couldn't quite bring myself to remind him that I was his son, so I mentioned my mother and focussed on why I was in Reykjavík—I had my roots here, I'd told him.

'Can I speak English?' I asked.

'No,' he replied, 'please speak Icelandic. I understand you. But where is your mother? Is she here with you?'

No. She was back in Brisbane. It had been her idea that I come to Reykjavík. She didn't want me to forget where I was from. And in any case, she'd said, I should have a year off between school and university—to travel, to breathe and, despite everything that had happened in the years before, to get in touch with my father. To find him, as she had done nearly twenty years before.

'We must meet,' he said, quietly and close, like a co-conspirator. 'There are some things I have to talk to you about. I'm in a difficult position.'

I suppose we both were, and I did want to meet him, but I had to explain that I was going away for a week, on a bus tour some old friends had organised for me. Our meeting would have to wait until I got back. I was annoyed with myself; I should have called earlier, when we could have met straight away.

The next day I joined a small group of travellers and we began our crossing of Sprengisandur, the wide, vacant tundra of Iceland's central highlands. I'd just spent two weeks of late nights hunched over a friend's typewriter, writing poems about a girl called Jessica, who I'd left behind in Scotland. It felt right to be among the long, desolate echoes of Iceland's geological past, and beyond myself. It suited my mood, which suddenly sought out open spaces, the sparse intensity of the island's interior. The blue mountains were always distant. White glacial rivers cut through the black hills of fine lava, ribbons of cream light on their way to the south coast.

Our guide mentioned the famous outlaws who'd survived in the tundra for years. They would steal sheep that had strayed from the farms of the fertile valleys to the north, once a wealthy part of the country but now losing out to the south. The sea, he said, was populated with benign creatures, generous-hearted seals that came to the aid of fishermen in distress. But the interior was only ever a feared and dangerous place—something like my father, I thought, and the mysteries of his interior life. A lost landscape. Farmers who crossed it on their way to markets perished, their deaths stored in the common imagination as a warning to others.

All the others on the bus were Icelandic and, over the three days it took us to cross the black tundra, the group task was to improve my grasp of the language. They sensed my falling away from Iceland; and as far as they were concerned being an Icelander meant speaking the language. 'It will come back,' they kept on reassuring me. Perhaps they sensed my hope that it would, for I had said nothing to them about wanting to return here.

They asked me about my story, my Icelandic side, and I gave them the poor return of well-rehearsed, evasive answers. But what was I doing in Australia? they asked, as though living in such a far-flung place signalled some deliberate perversity on my part. Didn't I want to come back to Iceland to live? Of course I did. That was the Icelandic gene, wasn't it; you could never stay away for long? You had to return to where you belonged, where you were known.

As always, the problem wasn't in forgetting where home was, but in working out a way of getting there. A month before, the Icelandic embassy in London had told me that, in the eyes of the law at least, I was a foreigner who simply happened to have been born in Iceland. My mother was English. There was nothing in the records to suggest an Icelandic connection.

I protested ineffectually, telling them I was born and raised in Reykjavík—didn't that mean something?

No. It might be different, they conceded, if I could get my father to acknowledge me. There had to be evidence of his paternity: 'You say your father is Icelandic, but there is no record of this.'

Technically, Ed Reid, my mother's ex-husband, was my father. She had still been married to Ed when I was born. Although my mother had refused to give a father's name for my birth certificate, the law had an alternative in Ed. To prove the point, I was shown a copy of my birth certificate. There was Ed Reid's name with a note in Icelandic that read, 'In the absence of a declaration of fatherhood, the mother's husband is deemed to be the father of the child.'

I could feel the humiliation of those words, or more particularly the sting of being surprised by what was on my birth certificate—still. I thought Gísli, my real father, might have changed his attitude after all these years, and he had the power to change that birth certificate. My mother had never made him out to be a villain. In fact, her stories about him were always flattering: he was successful and hard-working; he had a big, new house by the sea; his wife was beautiful; he could be charming and funny, especially when he talked about Iceland. He was as sentimental about his home as any nostalgic Icelander could be, and this was a country that specialised in the painful love of one's country. In Iceland, you could be homesick even when you were home.

Perhaps, I thought, he would see this in me, too, and bend in his resolve to stay quiet about me. He would recognise that my coming back to Iceland was never just a visit; it was a homecoming, another chance at immersing myself and finding, in the years ahead, the sense of belonging that existed in the past. But I needed his help. I needed him to say that I had a father here. Even if it were just for the two or three seconds it took him to sign a form.

When I got back from the north, I rang again. In the same torn Icelandic as our first conversation, I arranged to meet him at a car yard just down from where I was staying—just down from my room with the typewriter, the stack of poems, and the views over the southern shores of the town.

It was a five-minute walk through the damp September air. Fortunately, there weren't many people around, but in any case he and I knew each other straight away. He was tall, and more fallen away in the face than I'd expected; tired-looking. But the resemblance between us, which Mum had spoken about so often, was there: the light brown hair, the babyish cheeks, a small mouth, and eyes that disappeared when we smiled. I remember he wore a light brown jacket—it was the same colour as his four-wheel drive. The match gave him a middle-of-the-road flashiness.

We shook hands.

'*Velkominn heim,*' he greeted. (Welcome home.)

'*Takk,* Gísli,' I replied.

'I want to go for a drive,' he said straight away. 'There's somewhere I'd like to show you. And we can talk undisturbed in the car.'

We wound down to a road that skirted a small bay of skerries and tidal mudflats near the south road out of town. With the rising wind, there were little sailing boats out on the water.

'This back road is better, I think. No-one will see us here.'

It wasn't a promising start, but I'd heard so much about this fearfulness that the comment didn't surprise me. My mother had often said that he hadn't coped with the outcome of their affair. He had never allowed himself to be seen in public with us. Even the potted fjord sidetracks that we followed today were dangerous grounds for him.

I was strangely preoccupied with his appearance and didn't worry too much about his nerves. His looks had faded. I had a view on this: it was probably due to the worry that I might one day come back and claim something from him. How old was he? I didn't know, and even today, when I have more reason to know, I struggle to remember. He couldn't have been much more than fifty then.

'It's a small town, as you know,' he said, turning to me as he drove. 'I think people would guess who you were if they saw us together.'

I supposed he was right. We were so similar, and clearly the resemblance tortured him. He had been sure that it would one day undo our secret, and in a way he was right.

'Have you told anyone you're seeing me today?' he asked. 'I have to be careful.'

'Yes, one or two people, but no-one who knows you.' This was a lie. I had told Ragnar, one of his closest friends.

'Good,' he replied. 'That's very good.'

We bumped along an uneven track that brought us out at Álftanes, a flat, exposed spit on the other side of the bay. Beyond it was the open coastline of the Reykjanes peninsula, and the table mountains of the highlands to the south. He said he was taking me to Bessastaðir, the president's lodge and its cluster of farmhouses on the far side of Skerjafjörður.

'Have you been before?' he asked.

'No, never.'

'I worked there when I was a boy. You probably know that my father—your grandfather—died when I was young. I sometimes had to work to help Mother.'

Being fatherless was another thing we shared, I had always known that about us. I, too, had been doing odd jobs around Reykjavík when I was eight, but I didn't mention this to Gísli. I don't think I had ever helped much with the bills—my earnings went mainly on Matchbox cars.

'It's always windy here,' he continued. 'Wind and goose shit, and that's how I remember it.' It was cold, too, and it was just the two of us. No tour groups out today.

'Yes, I really worked here as a boy,' he said again, as we walked from the car.

'For your mother's sake?'

'Things were different when I was a boy. Everyone worked. Children worked all summer.'

'What's my grandmother's name?' I asked.

'Fríða Kristín Gísladóttir. She is very tough but a very good, kind woman—strong, like your mother.'

'Your grandfather's name is Gísli?'

'This is a family of family names. You are the exception.

But your mother chose well. You should be happy with Kári. It means "wind". Did you know that?'

I couldn't get him to speak English, so the conversation remained patchy. It seemed we wanted different things from this day, and perhaps that made things more awkward still. He told me he was fond of this place, and he walked around it in a ponderous mood that seemed to have little to do with my showing up. I guessed that the farm stood for his childhood, and that this made him uneasy. But, despite the language difficulties, I could see that, just as my mother had often said, he was a natural guide, personalising everything. I understood why she remembered and often quoted their talks about Iceland. His seriousness was attractive.

'We won't disturb her,' he said, pointing to the lodge. 'We are too polite for that.' He then said the president, Vigdís Finnbogadóttir, might well have been looking down on us, wondering who we were. Two tall, awkward men feeling the cold of the first days of winter, dodging goose shit and staying out when they should have gone in.

'It's funny. I used to push her trolley around,' I replied. 'We've both worked for the president.'

I liked all this: the wind, the cold, the revelations. He brought me here because it was deserted; but I interpreted it to also mean that he couldn't quite contain a second desire, which was to show off to his son, and perhaps even to relate me to Iceland.

'It's wonderful to be back in Iceland,' I confessed.

'Let's go back,' he said. 'We can talk better in the car.'

We got out of the wind and he began a light interrogation

that I had expected much earlier. He had waited until after we walked around together.

'Is there any reason you got in touch with me?' he asked. 'It's been such a long time since I saw your mother.'

He kept saying 'your mother' or 'Susan', and it occurred to me that fathers you grow up with call their wives 'mum'.

'No, no reason.' I tried to slow down my thoughts. I wanted him to think beyond the threat he thought I posed: 'Well, I wanted to meet you.'

The truth was, I didn't know why I was there. It had simply been a necessity. Perhaps I just wanted him. Perhaps I wanted this nervous man to line-up beside my much better, imagined version of him and take over. I wanted a better father than the one I had had till then. I wanted him to recognise himself in me, to be affected by our meeting, and to take this opportunity to be my father. And I wanted him to sign a simple form, and with that signature perform the most elemental declaration of all: this person comes from Susan Reid and Gísli Ólafsson. This person is ours. This boy is mine.

'Can you keep me a secret?' he asked, instead. 'My wife would leave me if she found out. I'd lose everything.'

He was embarrassed to be so nervous, I could tell. He was embarrassed that even a seventeen year old could see how much he had fretted over asking this question. How he had timed it.

'I didn't come here to cause any problems,' I replied. It was a line I had rehearsed over and over. 'But I have a question I want to ask you. It's rather personal.'

'Yes, go ahead.'

'Were you ever in love with my mother—I mean, when I was conceived?'

It feels like only yesterday when I asked this, and not twenty years ago. Even after all this time to dwell on it, I am still a little puzzled as to why I asked. Perhaps it was a test: if he loved her, then I was right about my mother, and she had loved him. It wasn't true then, as she liked to say, that there wasn't anything all that special about Gísli. I was sure you didn't love someone without having some of that love returned.

My father didn't look at me, but I could see he wasn't upset. I had thought he might refuse to answer. Instead, he kept his thin eyes focussed on the track ahead as he drove and I thought I detected a light smile in them. Then he replied, 'Yes, I loved your mother very much.'

I was delighted.

'In fact,' he continued, 'I only ever loved two women in my life. Your mother, Susan, and my wife. I have never told anyone that before.'

He was now talking as much to himself as he was to me. He wasn't exactly justifying himself; the mood was more nostalgic than defensive. He leant a shoulder towards the steering wheel as we cornered, as though for some kind of emphasis.

When we arrived back in town, he was reminiscing about Iceland in the 1970s, telling me how many of the roads we were driving along had been unpaved until long after my mother had arrived on the island. The concrete homes on the outskirts of town were all new, he said, the overflow of new money.

'Your mother probably wouldn't approve. She was rather pure about the old Iceland.'

'She still is. She loves the way it was when she first arrived. I think she would be disappointed to see all this development.'

'We all did love it. She came during a golden time. When we all woke up. When the country woke up.'

After a pause he asked, 'Isn't your birthday coming up?'

'Yes. I'll be eighteen this month.'

'I'm sorry I haven't sent you anything in the past.'

He stopped the car and unclipped a piece of paper from the sun visor and wrote down the date of my birthday.

'I'll try to remember better in the future.'

It was, I understood, his way of saying he didn't want to see me again.

'Is there anything I can help you with in Iceland?' he asked.

'I could use some help with money,' I surprised myself by asking. Yes, I was broke on this trip, and it would help to have some more cash for the travels that lay ahead. But I was also suddenly aware that my request was voicing a longer resentment about his money, and my mother's struggles over the years to get by.

'What for?'

It didn't occur to me that I'd need a reason for it. I gave him vague answers about university and travelling.

'It's tricky,' he replied. 'We're going to Spain soon. It's going to be an expensive trip.'

'It doesn't matter, then.'

'No, wait.' He offered me a couple of hundred dollars, saying we would have to drive to the bank to get it. 'Would that be all right?'

'Yes,' I said, 'that would be all right.' I also thought it would be humiliating and ridiculous. Why didn't I at least ask for a decent amount, something that looked like a request for help and not a failed extortion attempt?

He gave me the money, and we shook hands a second time.

'You won't tell anyone, then?' he asked.

'No,' I replied, 'you have my word.'

That promise came into being through my mother's kindness to Gísli. Eventually I broke it—I turned my back on Gísli's needs and, in a sense, on my mother's. But breaking that promise wasn't going to be an easy decision, and it would bring with it as many questions about the past as it did answers. It would also make me realise that you can only ever make your own way home.

1

THE SHARK NET AT BALMORAL

'Will you keep me a secret?' he asked. That was what he'd said on the night she told him she was pregnant; a dark, winter's night in the west side of Reykjavík in February 1972. Outside, the lawns were frosted over, brittle underfoot. Shadows crossed between the hazy arcs thrown by orange streetlights. Pedestrians scurried past and left behind them the cold scent of cigarettes and office dust.

Inside my mother's small basement apartment he reminded her, as he did me later on, that his wife would certainly leave him if she found out. A wife who had borne him five children. A devoted wife. He would be disgraced. The children would lose respect for their father. They would see his absences in a new way. They would know that they hadn't been because of hard work, but due to the philanderer's distance.

Then he wrote down his blood group on a scrap of paper and said, 'You'll need this.' Rather like, as eighteen years on, he wrote down my birthday—they were the only written records of my bloodline.

And my mother had agreed. She would bear the secret for both of them, and the responsibility for the affair, one that ended up lasting for seven years and which he always managed to keep from his family life and good reputation. She would protect him, and herself I suppose, from the implications of his paternity, the scandal. At seventeen, when he and I met in Reykjavík, I couldn't even overcome the feeling that he deserved our loyalty and protection still, and the feeling that the slight chance that might exist for us to be father and son depended on it. He was more likely to become a true father if I did as he wished.

As long as I could remember, I had wanted him to recognise and love me. That can't be surprising. Wasn't it just a basic, instinctual need for a father, intensified in my case by a desire for what I knew I couldn't have? From an early age I was aware he was beyond reach, and I was conscious my father's identity was a secret from all but me, my parents, and perhaps one other—my father's brother and only confidant, Pétur. I had grown up with this, and I was as committed to the secret as my mother. He was my father, but he was also my father only to me.

Another side of me, though, wondered why.

Why, really, were we so careful of his position in the world? Why had my mother promised to protect him, and why had she kept to her promise with such perseverance, even in the face of constant pressure from her friends, from officials and, eventually, from me to make Gísli face the consequences of the affair? And then, why had I agreed, all these years later, to keep to my part of the promise? Was I scared, as surely he was, of what would happen if my true identity were brought into the open? Was I really so afraid of losing him, a father I'd never had?

And then there is my mother. When I was five, she and I left Iceland for Sydney. My mother wanted to end the affair, and you couldn't get much further away from Gísli and Reykjavík than Sydney. That's what it took. Australia also represented a homecoming of sorts, as my mother's parents had migrated there from England when she was ten. It now became an opportunity for a fresh start in an old haunt—to be clear of Gísli and perhaps find someone new, a father figure for me. She ended the affair by leaving Iceland. She would, like me, spend the rest of her life looking for ways to go back.

Even in the relatively quiet days of 1977, Mosman was genteel and a little off to the side of what was really going on. Military Road, which branched off the main street north out of central Sydney, descended with snobby leisure into the Mosman shops until it seemed that you'd reached a town apart, an enclave of middle-class Australianisms: the milk bar, the bowls club with a view of the harbour, and what I recall as a scrubby, dusty school on a corner opposite a cricket oval that was always parched, always needed sprinkling. In its gradual descent to a terminus of suburban busyness, it was like the main street leading down to the centre of Reykjavík, except dry, warm, and friendly.

My mother recognised all this as the customary features

of an Australia that hadn't changed since she'd left seven years before. The plot points were more or less the same as they had been in Macksville, a little town in central New South Wales where she'd lived as a girl. That wasn't the real issue, though. In the intervening years a lot had happened to her. She'd had a long affair with a married man and now she had brought a half-Icelandic son to live in a still-unworldly Australia.

As in Reykjavík, the talk of being cosmopolitan was entirely for the benefit of the locals, who alone noticed the minute indictors of the new and the foreign. Foreigners didn't notice anything except the Australian conservatism, still strong and rude—little had changed. After living in a country devoted to children, even those of secrets and scandals, the frowns now directed at my mother as a single mother were a shock. She was not to be taken in to the polite circles of the North Shore.

Instead, we lingered on Reykjavík time, and ticked along to a consciousness that was always about going back to the north, one day. To the other city of light and water, which is what they had in common. Sydney and Reykjavík were ports with 'names for the sea', as W.H. Auden had written. In my mind, they were always twin cities, long since separated but aware of each other.

But for my mother, even though she knew she needed to get away from Gísli and, even with roots in Australia, there was no understanding about why she'd come back. She hadn't even settled into her new job before she was planning our next departure. It was so like her father, Harold, who had never been able to put down roots. But unlike Harold, who was unhappy until his death, my mother knew where she belonged. She wasn't lost, like him. No. She was a true exile. It was always Iceland, because she couldn't ever be finished with it. In the meantime, it was Mosman. It was the steep walk down to Balmoral Beach. White Ford Falcons. Storms on the way home in the afternoon. The navy grey of stone walls. The paper brown of trees.

For my own part, I had decided that Mum ought to marry—I knew, already, that the real problem was that we were missing someone, and the key, I realised, was men. You had to find them and then approach them, neither of which seemed to come naturally to her. So, I did it. Normally, I spoke to the ones sitting on their own on busses or trains, on the ferry benches or at parks. They weren't always the ones that an adult would pick. There was a simple procedure I followed. I pointed at Mum and said, 'Do you think that lady over there is pretty?' Feigning good will, most men said, 'Yes'.

'Would you like to marry her?' I would then ask, moving in a single movement towards my goal. My success rate was low, and Mum didn't appreciate my efforts, at all. But how else was she going to find a husband?

We lived on the middle floor of a three-storey apartment block, and I confided in our upstairs neighbour, Carline, and our downstairs neighbours, Peter and Mary, that Mum was a hopeless case. I also related another key piece of information, which was that, according to Mum, she'd had enough of men.

'Don't you think that's a silly thing to say?' I asked Carline.

'Well, you men are quite something,' she replied to her six-year-old interrogator.

'Why?'

'The thing about men, Kári, is that they seldom mean anything they say.'

'Are they liars?'

'No, not exactly liars. They want too much, that's all.'

Carline was unreliable. Like my mother, she had been surprised to find herself back in Australia. Her return had come at the end of many years in London where, she always said—and as I have heard so many Australians say since—she felt more at home than she'd ever felt in Sydney.

'We can't decide where to live,' she explained to me. 'It doesn't help if you love Australia, because loving a place isn't enough. But your mother is a natural homemaker. Your apartment looks much more cosy than mine, and you two have only just arrived. What do you think of that?'

'Why did you come back, then?' I asked.

'Because of my mother,' she replied. 'My mother was very sick. But then she lived and lived and lived. And when she died, it was too late to go back again.'

'Why was it too late?'

'Because the man I should've stayed for hadn't waited long enough. He wasn't patient.'

'Weren't you married?'

'No. I missed my chance. But that's a while ago now.'

'Are you sick of men, too?'

'Oh, no. I am not sick of men. And nor is your mother. We've got you, haven't we?'

There. They weren't sick of men. This was crucial. It meant, of course, that my search must go on. There were nice teachers at Mosman Primary School. Then there was Marco at the milk bar. He'd looked after the twenty dollar note I'd found until, three months on, no-one had claimed it.

'Kári, the whole of Mosman doesn't need to know that I'm not married,' said Mum.

'But how else will they know?' I replied.

'Know what?'

What I wanted the whole world to know, it seems: that there was no particular reason for us being fatherless. Mum was no different to other mothers. With the right man, she might even be cured of her restlessness, even of her attachment to Iceland. We would settle in Mosman. What I wanted all of the world, and most especially Mosman, to see was that Mum was ready to be loved. What I hadn't yet come to realise about her, was the fact that it was love that stood in the way of love. It had begun to stand in my way, too.

Already, at six, my relations with the opposite sex were fraught. I was being confined to a month of lunches under the big tree at school, the penalty for throwing stones at girls. Boys were different. You could throw all the stones you liked at them. Mosman Primary, I was discovering, had an inflexible attitude to the pleasures in life. They didn't like it when you raced across the next-door oval while it was being sprinkled. They didn't like it when I talked in class, which even today—as a lecturer in English—I believe is the main function of a class. And they didn't like it if I made quacking noises with my cheeks, which, along with playing with the knots at the end of a duvet cover, had become an addiction.

My grandmother, Mildred, came for a visit and mended

the torn ends of my duvet cover. She also stuck her finger into my cheek whenever I began quacking.

'Don't do that, Grandma,' I insisted. 'Don't poke me.'

'Well, stop quacking, then.'

'But I like it.'

'Whatever made you think that was an excuse for anything? You think you can do things just because you like them?'

I see now it was the answer she must have practised on her husband, Harold, many times before. She must have been hard in her day. In its prima facie seriousness, her face was as Yorkshire as ever. She was still a nurse from Doncaster. But her face had crumpled in that Australian way. They weren't laughter lines, exactly. More crease marks created over the years as her face had slipped and left behind a memory of its old harsh self. It was now a good, kind face. We were friends from the start.

Between my mother and Mildred, though, tensions begun years before. As a girl, my mother sided with her father Harold and his restlessness. Mildred and my mum now found it hard to talk to each other, and Mum would be relieved when Mildred's visits ended. But I understood my grandmother— the main thing for her was to feel at home—and I couldn't imagine why Mum didn't like her as much as I did. Mildred and I would sit on our balcony overlooking the car park and watch the traffic go by on our street without any sense of restlessness at all. The passing cars were, to us, just passing cars: they weren't necessarily going anywhere.

As I came out to join her on the balcony one day Mildred yelled, 'Don't close that!' But I had. The door shut and locked.

It was only midmorning and Mum wouldn't be home until five-thirty.

'What are we going to do until then?' cried Mildred.

'We can talk,' I replied.

'Talk! It's all right for you. You can pee over the side. What about me? Where am I going to go?'

'You can go over the side, too,' I replied.

An hour passed.

'Call out to him,' Mildred said, pointing at a young man walking along the pavement. But she took over. 'Would you let us in? The front door's unlocked. Just come around and open the balcony door for us.'

He walked upstairs and slid open the balcony door.

'Thank you,' I said.

'You talk to him, Kári. I'm going to the loo.'

Naturally, I told him all about my mother.

No-one ever swam within the shark net at Balmoral Beach. It was a gothic-looking apparatus, a sea monster. Sydney Harbour might well have been full of sharks but Mum, for one, had been swimming in open water since she was a girl. Her philosophy, along it seemed with all the other residents of Mosman and Balmoral, was that it was better to be taken in clear water than to swim safely in the trapped effluent of the nets. The rest of the beach was so clean and bright. This was Sydney, after all, a glorious stretch of Australian brightness. As Clive James promised, the sharks only ever took one person at a time.

My mother couldn't quite bring herself to adopt the same good will in relation to men. No matter my efforts, she had sworn off them, and she hadn't really trusted another man since we moved to Sydney. Gísli was hardly a shark, but he had done enough to keep her in the shallows. My efforts failed. Over the years, she would often give reasons for staying single. Men didn't like it when they saw she had a child, or men preferred younger women; and, no doubt, she was right about a lot of men. But, in truth, I don't think she ever tried very hard to meet anyone. She would remain single, like Gísli in a way, who had allowed a part of himself to become a single man in a marriage.

I say it was love. Surely, love can only ever be a good, worthwhile thing, but for Mum it was complex, full of inner conflict and guilt, and she was never going to be able to limit its impacts. Their love meant that it would always be just me and my mother, a lone parent with a lone child, both to some extent supported by the promise made to Gísli, and the promise of Iceland that it offered. We kept our connection to both.

'Do you like it here?' Mum asked me. I was seven, and it would be hard not to like living by the beach. But my mother's old boss in Iceland wrote and asked her to come back to the firm, the one she had worked for when she started her new life in Iceland ten years before. They offered to pay for us both to come back.

'I'm thinking that we should maybe go back to Iceland,' she said. 'I do miss it.'

'Okay.'

'You won't mind?'

'It won't matter, Mum, as long as we're together.'

That, says Mum, was enough to seal it. She would take us back to Iceland, back to where her thoughts had been tending since we'd left two years before. It was time for her to try again.

2

THE ROAD TO REYKJAVÍK

It's a long way from Australia to Iceland, but then my mother, Susan Joan Diggons, had always dreamt of being as far away as possible. Like her father Harold, she was the sort who was never entirely satisfied; the one who needed to get away before she felt like she was reaching home. So why not Iceland? That's how it went with her—'Well, why not?'—and then the decision to move was made.

It's one of the things I like most about her. In that nonchalance existed a type of bravery I have often wished I had more of myself. In me, it comes paired with my father's sense of caution. In my mother, it was a replacement for other kinds of courage that she didn't have. She could be achingly shy. And it could also cloak more serious attachments, especially in the case of Reykjavík. We weren't going back just because there had been a letter from her old employers in Iceland. We were going back because she thought she had found a solution to her restlessness.

She had been shifting about constantly, more or less, since

she was ten. This was when her family—the Diggons—migrated from their modest, unsettled life in Berkshire to Thumb Creek, then a desperately vacant valley in central New South Wales, about an hour's drive from the coastal town of Macksville. Harold had great hopes in the migration—a chance to escape the disappointments of postwar England.

But they felt Australia was hostile and unpromising, and much inferior to what they'd left. Perhaps in 1951 it was. Susan shared in her father's distress; the very day after they arrived in Thumb Creek, she solemnly swore to herself that she would leave the first chance she had. It happened like this.

She was set atop an old horse called Bluey, of all things, and was told to follow a thin track winding through a valley of creek beds to Thumb Creek School. She was scared. She was shy. She was awkward about being tall for her age. She knew she seemed foreign to others, as indeed she would be from then on, no matter where she lived. She was not Australian. She was already not quite English, either. The world around her was menacing, and she loathed the idea of joining a new school. But within her she had something that she'd discovered on the voyage from England.

A few weeks before they had been merely names and illustrations in her geography textbook. But during the journey out, during those exquisite hours she spent alone on deck watching the passing shoreline, the treasured information in her schoolbooks had been transported into the uneven, chaotic outlines of ports. Real ports. They were her future.

Again, that line from Auden fits: the 'ports have names for the sea'.

Bluey stopped by a small timber building and Mum dismounted. There was no-one outside, but she heard the sound of shoes and bare feet echo among the trees. She stood for a minute, reigns in hand, thinking someone might appear. When no-one did, she chose a tree by the side of the schoolhouse to tie up the horse.

'You'll have to wait for me here,' she said. 'Wait here, Bluey.'

She whistled her way to the school house—apparently, it kept away the snakes—and walked in.

Mr Jason Savage, a handsome teacher of no more than twenty, introduced himself and the class, most of whom belonged to one family, the Kirkmans. Mr Savage wore shorts and long socks. He sat her at a desk roughly suited to her height, or only a little smaller, and asked her what she'd seen during the trip to Australia.

'The Pyramids,' she replied.

'In that case,' said Mr Savage, 'let's have a day in Egypt.' I wonder what would have happened had he not indulged his new student in this way. I know from my own experiences that the one consolation of a new school is being not only novel but exotic. It was a consolation that could become a little addictive.

In the time it had taken her to ride from the farm to school, Susan learnt that a way out of feeling alone was to capture again, even in memory, the sensation of living that she felt in those ports: how they gave her contact with the wider world, its romance, and its distance from the everyday. It was to these ports and others like them that she promised herself a return. After school, the ride home was better for my mother but her resolve was strong. She never wavered from that promise to herself. Not after school, and not now, nearly sixty years later.

The warmth of the afternoon had soaked into the track, releasing insects and the green sweetness of the grass. Bluey, recognising that he was close to home, cantered along the track. It was Australian optimism: get home, have a feed, rest. When she saw her father at the front door, she released all the fears of the morning, jumped off Bluey and ran in crying. 'I don't want to go back to school,' she wept.

Harold was feeling as unsettled as his daughter. It had been a mistake to come out to Australia; that much was clear to him. In the end, they managed just six weeks at Thumb Creek before they followed the track and its cows to the coast. They bought a small house in Macksville, on the north bank of the Nambucca River on the edge of a highway that ran from Brisbane to Sydney. Across the river stood the Star Hotel, the cinema, and the milk bar—the compass of urban experience in the 1950s.

In front of the house, the traffic hummed an irresistible tune to both father and daughter. They knew there was more: you just had to follow the cars out of town. Four years later they did, to Sydney and a return passage back to England.

It was a disaster, just as it had been a mistake to move to Australia in the first place. Like so many immigrants, Harold was tricked by unreliable memories; firstly of home and then of the new country. Within weeks of landing back in England he told a disconsolate family that he was homesick for Australia. They would, he said, have to make a second migration.

'I've had just about enough of you looking for somewhere you like,' said Mildred.

'England's changed. It's not what it was when we left.'

England hadn't changed, she replied, and nor had he. She felt it was just his way of saying that family life wasn't enough. Or, that this family wasn't the one he wanted. They argued bitterly, Harold always convinced that the next step in his life would be the defining one. He was, though, made to wait by a force greater than Mildred. Australia was as popular then as it is now, and it took nine months for Harold to find a passage back to Sydney.

As they were in-between homes and countries, Harold and Mildred thought there was no point in their daughter going to school. Instead, when she was fifteen Susan Diggons took a clerical job at the local council, and at night she went to secretarial school. It was a strict, dry kind of education—typing speeds and shorthand symbols—but in those days a very useful one. It would one day get her a job in Reykjavík.

On their return to Australia, the family moved to Wollongong where, perhaps inevitably, Harold and Mildred separated. They had, it seemed, moved across the world just to split up. He found somewhere to stay near the sea, Mildred took a job at a boarding school and moved there with my mother's sister, Lee, who was younger and closer to Mildred. My mother was found a bed at a women's hostel. At sixteen, she was on her own, a state which from then on she would return to as a home of sorts, a corollary and yet also an alternative to being let down by the ones you loved. Being alone is the natural companion of change.

My mother's full escape arrived three years later. It came in the form of the Australian Navy and the man declared by Icelandic law to be my father, Ed Reid. A year after she joined up, she married him. She was nineteen and felt she was on her way at last.

Ed was handsome and very Australian: grinning, a lot of facial hair, thin, an adventurer—he'd trained as a radio operator and wanted to go on expeditions; his hero was Douglas Mawson. Shortly after their wedding he left for Antarctica. A year later he returned with sketches of emperor penguins and news of a rocky outcrop named in his honour.

Perhaps symptomatic of the era, while he travelled she stayed at home and waited. She spent a year with the in-laws and managed to save one thousand pounds. But she had fallen for someone even less steady than her father. As if to prove it, the day after he came home, Ed spent six hundred pounds on a Kombi van, and off they went. Away from Sydney and the in-laws.

It was a good marriage, though, and in many ways a fulfilling one for Mum, who from then on joined Ed on all his outdoor jobs—in the Snowy Mountains, Kangaroo Valley, on the Hawkesbury River. She had found someone to travel with, and she was in love. The ports she'd met in the journeys from England faded a little in her memory because it was enough to simply be with a man who saw the world as you did and moved around a lot. 'Why not?' they said in unison. It was the 1960s after all. There were always jobs going, no matter where you went. Live freely. The creed of a decade was a revelation for Ed but Mum had been living what other people called 'free' all her life. She didn't need much convincing to believe that the wanderer's life was the best one going. Home was always somewhere else. Later on, she wasn't so sure.

She was twenty-six when Ed told her that he'd met someone else—someone, of course, who understood him better than she had. It was the worst moment in her life and she couldn't eat or sleep. When she talks about their separation, she always remembers her first sleep after Ed left, a full two weeks later, and her first, very plain sandwich—all she could eat when she could again stomach food. But his departure reunited her with a sense of self-reliance that she'd formed when her parents had separated a decade before. Places mattered, people left.

As it was a childless marriage—they couldn't have children together—and because Ed couldn't stand the idea of a mortgage, there was no property to divide. Just the Kombi. For a young woman in the mid 1960s, when most were stuck at home while their husbands were working and having affairs, she found herself relatively free. She now felt she had a second chance to take off, to do something she'd been promising herself since she was ten, and she grabbed it. She just went, like Harold and, it seemed, Ed had.

First, she went to Lord Howe Island, a crater mass miles out to sea from Sydney. Then, Mount Cook in New Zealand. By June 1969, three years before my birth, the impulse had taken her as far as Nakhodka on the east coast of Russia, where she boarded the Trans-Siberian train for Moscow. She was heading for England, this time on her own.

It was fourteen years since she'd been in England as a teenager learning shorthand and typing, but the charm of the place was still there, layered and, as always, to some extent hidden—the hedgerows and the summer evenings, the polite irony of odd conversations at bus stops, English television. It was all as good as everyone had reminded her, and as fresh as she remembered. Even her childhood friends were true. She began looking for work.

My guess is that at this time she was already thinking about where to go next. But the story she tells is that the next step took her by surprise. It was an advertisement in *The Times* that stated, 'English-speaking secretary wanted for Iceland. Twenty-five pounds per week, no tax'. It was only two lines in a broadsheet, but it was enough. The following Monday she rang the number in the paper and was talking to an employment agent who couldn't believe anyone would ever want to go to Iceland. A week later, Mum had signed up for her first winter.

She was met by the representative of T & J—or G. Thorsteinsson & Jónsson, importers, in the full version—a young man who held my mother's arm and led her urgently to the car. Through experience she had become independent, and the country with which she was about to fall in love valued independence, probably above all things. She was at her most beautiful, with straight, black hair down to her waist—something like the most famous Viking princesses who, a thousand years before, had come to Iceland from the far corners of the old Norse world, Sweden, Russia, Scotland and even the north of England. But, like most travellers, she was lonely. She didn't really believe herself when she said that your own company was the best. And perhaps, most importantly for me, she had grown used to unreliable men.

'Welcome to Iceland,' yelled the representative, as they walked through the car park. The wind picked up, as it almost always does at such moments in Iceland—during arrivals and departures—and they began to run.

'You have come at a very vindy time of year.'

'Is December particularly bad?' my Mum asked.

'Yes. But it can be quite nice in July.'

They drove in the half-light of a winter's afternoon. On one side, the lava field ran without interruption to a ridge of dark craters; on the other, the grey ocean surged. Farm buildings stood isolated, as if unattached to the small fields around them. Thirty minutes later, the aluminium smelter, with its high tower painted in barber shop stripes of red and white, appeared—the first indication that you were getting close to the town of Hafnajörður and, just beyond it, the capital. When they arrived in Reykjavík, Mum was dropped off with her suitcase at a basement apartment.

'This is Sólvallagata,' said the driver. 'Quick. Get in out of the vind.'

Before she did, she looked down along her new street, an elegant arc of four-storey buildings. It was a lovely street. The next day, when the wind had settled down a bit, she discovered the street ran towards a gorgeous, small town that was unspoilt, unpolluted, and undeveloped. This was before the economic miracle had really taken hold of Iceland.

In December 1970, there was just a single supermarket for the whole country.

Mum found the people were in a way like her: quiet. And just like farmers, they took the time to explain things, even though they were all working two or three jobs—a habit they hadn't managed to leave behind on the farms of the old days. For the first time in her life, Mum felt understood, as these people liked her quietness, her self-reliance, and also what was, I suppose, her paradoxical willingness to be adopted, to be taken into a culture that made you wait. The idea that you could be more yourself by moving had happened.

Icelanders might be quiet and therefore difficult to know, but now and then they were prepared to reveal an inner voice that resonated with her, a lost-in-the-world irony and dislocation. They had a delicate wit that was self-deprecating, time-tested, and rural. Many of them made her giggle, despite her being the non-giggly kind.

She quickly discovered one thing you could always do in Iceland, no matter the weather: swim. Like so many foreigners in Iceland, Mum fell in love with the outdoor swimming pools, where a steady steam rose from the depths. They had given the town its name—Reykja-vík, the 'bay of smoke'. The water was piped miles from its source deep underneath the heaths to the south. The sulphurous stink of the hot springs were a reminder in the urban world of the villages and farm clusters where everyone had once lived, and it provided much needed time outside.

These hot spots, along with formal coffee time, were provincial rituals that gave everyone the chance to fill in what the countless biographies of a polite, desperately small society left out: the illicit world of the Reykjavík cycle of affairs. They weren't exactly meant to happen—this was a conservative, Lutheran place after all. But the cold being the cold, the darkness being the darkness, and the familiarity being so intense, affairs were inevitable, and rather common. There was even something of a local tradition of forgiving them. What did a scandal matter if, at the end of it all, there was another child in the world? It wasn't a universal view—my father certainly didn't share it—but it was still the dominant one.

Among the local people, my Mum stood out. If she had looked English, she might have seemed less different. But, as Ed had liked to joke, everything about her was becoming more and more Italian—she didn't look Doncaster with her olive skin, black hair that ran far down her back, glamorous legs, deep eyes, and good nose. Gísli noticed her straight away and tried to catch her eye in the coffee room.

He was the charmer in the office, and so not at all my mother's type, she told me. She thought he was handsome in his way—you could tell that he thought he was good looking. Dashing and, like me I suppose, a touch vain. But, all the same, she couldn't see what all the fuss was about, why the other women in the office made him out to be something special. What caught her notice then?

'I was lonely and he was clean,' she said.

It's a joke, yes, and very much a Mum kind of joke, full of dismissal of higher emotions or the rhetoric of love. Unlike me, Mum wouldn't ever voice an appeal to the moon for inspiration—perhaps there was no moonlight in Iceland that year. From the photographs I have seen, Gísli did seem hand-some. Well, in those days, he looked like me; of course she fell for him.

As it turned out, she was about to fall in love with another one of those men with a destination he didn't quite understand himself—another Harold, another Ed; another man she could never really have. From what little I know of him, I would say that Gísli was, in fact, just loud enough to catch her eye from under her shyness, and whimsical enough to conceal from her that she was falling in love with one of those loud, charming ones she'd never much liked.

3

LOVE IN THE TIME OF COD WAR

Maybe, it was just the smell of cod in the air, an ichthyo-logic aphrodisiac. In the 1970s, Iceland was more concerned with the Cod Wars than the Cold War. Comical-sounding affairs, but they were achieving their ends. The enemy was the English, who were barging in and stealing fish like all the cod thieves before them: the Danes, the French, the Dutch, and the Spanish, each of them taking turns to exploit the fisheries while the locals were made to stand by the shore and watch. Not any more.

'This won't do!' declared a fuming Minister for Fisheries. It was time for war. And so the trawlers, armed with massive net-clippers, fought it out in a series of North Atlantic battles between a few Icelandic patrol boats and the Scots' fishing fleet. Against all probability, the Icelanders won and claimed more than their share of the fishing grounds.

After centuries as a nation of starving peasants and drown-ing fishermen, Iceland was now becoming wealthy. There were even cod millionaires, or 'quota millionaires' as they became known locally—they sold their small fishing quotas to the bigger operators and then retired, bored, to the higher streets of town. With the fish, Iceland became a proper nation. A nation of singing fishermen. In the course of three wars, spanning from 1958 to the years after my birth, they won the fisheries, and this was how the Iceland of my childhood became the Iceland of new money.

Before that, though, Gísli must have been planning his own international manoeuvre for some time. One evening, when he and my Mum were both working late, he asked if he could walk her home. They passed Bárugata, which he told her was his mother's street, the street of his childhood. Even in his youth, Gísli was sentimental. The area hadn't changed much since his boyhood years, he told Mum. Vesturbær, the oldest part of town, still looked like a Norwegian fishing village. They were near the harbour, and he told her about how he'd worked on the trawlers fifteen years before.

'Were things so bad in the old days that children had to work on the boats?' she asked him, as he was too young, surely.

'Well, at the time I saw myself as a young man.'

'Not at ten!'

'No, not at ten. I was nearly twenty.'

'But you don't seem much more than that now.'

'Oh, thank you, Susan. You're very kind. I turn thirty-five this year.'

She hadn't meant to compliment him, and she stumbled for a way of taking it back, before remembering that nothing was going to happen, anyway. She was more or less resigned to that. They'd reached Öldugata, a narrow street of apartments.

'Just up there,' said Gísli, 'is Ferðafélag Íslands and the Icelandic Touring Club. You should get up into the highlands,' he went on. 'That's where you go to become a real Icelander.'

'Whatever makes you think that I want to be a real Icelander?' she replied.

'I don't think you realise what a big city Reykjavík is,' he replied. 'You only get lost in Reykjavík. The country is where you get found.'

'Well, I think I'll find my own way from here,' she said. 'This is where I turn off.'

'Okay, Susan. Goodnight. And thank you for the walk.'

Gísli followed the road down to the ocean front while my mother headed the other way, towards Sólvallagata, the street of her basement apartment. She turned around to catch a last look at him. Yes, there was something there: the fisherman's charm turned urban.

The next morning, when she took the cover off her IBM golf ball typewriter, she found a Ferðafélag Íslands touring programme for the summer wedged under. How quickly he had worked her out. That evening, he followed her home. She knew he was there, and she allowed herself the odd glance at him. He threw a snowball.

'Stop that!' she called.

'Where are you going, Susan?' asked Gísli in reply.

'Home, of course.'

'Why would anyone want to go inside on a day like this? Let's have a snowball fight.'

'Don't you have somewhere to go?'

'I always have somewhere to go, Susan. You know, I'm a

very busy man. My brother's expecting me.' But instead of going to dinner with his brother, Pétur, he went to Susan's apartment. And that, as far as I can tell, was that.

Over the years I have made numerous unsuccessful attempts to learn more from my mother. This was surely a crucial moment in light of what was to follow. But there was no seduction, not unless you count snowballs. There was humour and lightness. And he came to her. It was the start of a relationship that might easily have begun only after months of flirtation, teasing, and nervousness, but instead it rolled on from a couple of conversations and two walks home. He was just what my mother needed—a charming local who might help her turn her back completely on England and Australia, and seal the end of her marriage to Ed. He might even help her forget Ed altogether.

For a long while, their affair would continue in the same, uncomplicated way. They seldom talked about the relationship, or reflected on its meaning for their lives outside my mother's small apartment in Sólvallagata—they only ever met there. In a way, I don't think he was even quite real, yet, for my mother—he was an Icelandic man in the early 1970s, surely something a little short of reality. He was more Reykjavík than reality. More light than landscape.

When my mother asked him why he wasn't married, he replied with blank surprise that he was. He had assumed she'd known—didn't everyone? Well, no, he didn't wear a wedding ring. That was because when he was on the trawlers it had got caught and nearly ripped his finger off. He had never worn one since. He seemed unperturbed, unanalytical about this revelation that had just entered their relationship, turning it into an affair.

Only once did he tell her a story about himself that sounded something like an allegory for what they were doing, or at least what unsettled him about it. It was a moment in his boyhood when he'd been sent by his mother to buy bread from the local bakery. He held the bread in one hand, and his change in the other. On his way home an earthquake hit, which was fairly common in Iceland. This time, though, it was more severe than the normal tremors. He was thrown to the ground. Everything was moving—the bakery, the road, the street signs. But the main crisis was this: which hand to put out to soften the fall?

'What did you save, the bread or the money?' my mother asked. It was, he'd answered, a moment of indecision that still bothered him.

But although Gísli wasn't troubled by guilt, he was nervous. As time went on, it became clear that he didn't really know how to balance the two sides of his life, that of a responsible family man and of the charmer who always wanted more. My mother began to hear about his wife and how drastic her reaction would be if she ever found out. She would leave him, take the kids, or even come after Mum. But as long as they could keep the affair a secret, everything would be okay.

She probably should have ended it the minute she found out he was cheating on his wife. It was wrong to be seeing a married man. But she couldn't resist the feeling that it was quite nice that he was taken. It spared her the troubles of ownership, of marriage. She wasn't his, not his to look after, or worry about, or impress. Ed had left her for someone more like himself, someone with things to say. A statement person. With Gísli, it was acceptable not to reflect. All he wanted was to be with her, to visit her apartment every now and then. And he made her laugh.

Suddenly, the charm that seemed forced looked crafted exclusively for her. He was her personal guide, and a way into Iceland that was touched not only with insight but also an intense love for the country and deep sentiment for the past. The people, he explained, were taciturn but profound; they were material but had good taste and family was everything, but most people couldn't really stand their relatives. Most of all, Icelanders were nostalgic for Iceland. It was a national hobby. Whatever you did, he warned her, you mustn't ever fall in love with Iceland. You would then never leave, not really.

She replied that she'd found her home here. She'd understood the place before she knew anything about it, before even his lectures began.

'What do you see?' he asked.

'Mount Esja, of course. And the light, like everyone says. It's so beautiful. I can walk and walk here. It's the most stunning landscape I have ever seen. And I feel right. It's hard to explain, but I'm in the right place here.'

'But surely Australia is very beautiful, too?'

'It is. But this is my landscape. I should have been born in Iceland.'

She had two destination points now, Reykjavík and the affair, both of which took her further away from her origins in England and Australia, and away from Harold and Mildred, and from Ed and her failed marriage. And perhaps one of the reasons my mother was so accepting of his need for secrecy, was that it meant that their meetings remained as another place to escape to, a further destination within Iceland. She had a companion and a new country, and both were miles away from those who'd known her before. Neither Gísli nor Iceland had any claim on her. This, I think, liberated her to fall in love with both.

Each year in April, the Icelandic newspapers celebrate the arrival of the Arctic Tern, or *kría*, my mother's favourite bird. It journeys all the way from the waters of the Antarctic, and yet arrives with all the purity and precision of spring. After months of cold and darkness, the Arctic Terns announce with their shrill cries and diving attacks that life has begun again in earnest. A window is opened, and out of it there comes a different country, freed of its coats and given back to the outdoors.

For Susan Reid, it was the signal to begin her travels around Iceland. On the weekends, she worked her way through the day trips listed in the Ferðafélag Íslands booklet that Gísli had left under her typewriter. And in July, when T & J closed for its summer break, she joined another migration, when half of Reykjavík, including Gísli and his family, either boarded charter flights to Spain, Italy or the resort towns of Tito's Yugoslavia, or went back into the country, to the fishing villages and farms where they'd grown up, and where they were needed for the summer work.

She had been counselled by Gísli to get out of Reykajvík and into the soul of the country, the bays, farmlands, and the rivers. Then, by chance, someone at T & J mentioned the Hafskip cargo ship that circumnavigated the island, taking on board a small number of paying passengers. The following day, she asked the firm's young messenger boy, Jón, to run down to the Hafskip offices to see what he could find out about it. He came back with a one-page schedule. Two ships operated at the same time, one following a clockwise, the other an anti-clockwise route.

It was an easy choice: the clockwise ship was called *The Esja*, named after the table mountain she so often watched from the Reykjavík shoreline. She and Jón traced the route on the map. Twenty-two stops in all, the whole country as the fishermen saw it, without once having to travel on the dirt roads. She immediately sent Jón back to the harbour with the money to pay for her passage.

That afternoon, he returned with a ticket and the news that he had bought one for himself, as well.

'Jón, you are joking, aren't you?' she said.

'Of course not,' replied Jón. 'Don't you want me to come?'

She didn't really need another one looking to her for some support for their own self-examination, but neither did she have the heart to turn him down. On the day of departure, as she stepped out of her taxi and looked up to the deck of the ship, there was Jón leaning on the handrails, waving down to her with all the excitement of a first-time traveller.

Below decks, she found her cabin, which she was to share with a German nurse, Annette, who was working in Reykjavík. They steamed into a cool day. A fog had settled over Faxaflói, the wide expanse of ocean to the north of the capital, and for the first hours of the trip Susan and Annette lay on their bunks reading. There wasn't anything to see. Then Jón stuck his head through the door, and smiled.

'Susan, do you have a cigarette?' he asked. She pulled out a packet from her bag and handed him one. Jón left.

'I'm not sure you should be giving those to a mere boy,' said Annette.

A few minutes later he reappeared.

'Susan, do you have match?'

Annette scowled. Mum passed him a match. He returned yet again.

'Oh, Jón, what is it now?' she asked.

'Do you have a camera?'

'Yes, I have a camera,' Mum replied. 'Why?'

'I want to take a picture.'

'Goodness me, Jón. There's nothing to see.'

'I want to take a picture of Snæfellsjökull for you. You're always saying how much you like it.'

'But the fog, Jón.'

'The fog's gone.'

They ran up on deck. They had crossed Faxaflói and were rounding Snæfellsnes, a long peninsula that reached out from the mid-west of the island. At its tip was Snæfell, a famous volcano; a crested, glacial summit that my mother often watched magnified in the low winter light of Reykjavík. To this day, it remains her emblem mountain of Iceland, an island littered with volcanic shells.

'I can take the pictures if you like,' said Jón.

'Thank you, Jón. Yes, please do.'

'You're very lucky to the see the peak,' Jón's new friend on deck, Indriði, said. 'Normally, it's covered in clouds.'

They were nearing the Westfjords, where the mountains fell into the sea like splayed book covers, and left little space for people. Most often, the small farming and fishing communities were pushed out onto thin, curving spits. These were the *eyri* in Vatneyri, Thingeyri, Flateyri and Suðureyri, villages that sat too close to the shore. The roads were edged into the mountainsides, making dark, uneven scars on the landscape. A very occasional car made sense of these wounds, but the roads were also popular with sheep, which rested on the warm surface of the gravel.

In the afternoons, my mother sat in the sun at the stern, on a bench that ran along the top of the life raft boxes. As she did, she watched the peninsulas pass by, each its own peculiar Esja for a village or a collection of white-walled farms. At the country's north-western extreme, they saw farms now all but abandoned and used only in the summers, when the grandchildren of the old farmers returned for hiking and berry picking.

Next they cruised back along the south coast and Vatnajökull, a glacier which, on a map, colours in the island's south-eastern corner; and Höfn, a harbour town on the low belly of Iceland's animal shape. She laughed as she tried to pronounce it.

'Just say it as if you're hiccuping,' said Jón.

The ever-changing landscape of a volcanic island, and the precarious habitations that occupied it were Mum's introduction to the Iceland of old, as it existed only in the outlying districts. I've often wondered how much of her time on board was taken up with thoughts of the capital, and the man who lived there. I'm quite sure that she would say, 'Oh, not much'—she would resist the movement to sentiment and drama. Still, she must have watched the coastline at least in part through his eyes. It was Gísli, after all, who'd told her to escape Reykjavík. He'd promised her that she'd find her Icelandic side there, and that was true. The landscape and the light pulled her in even more. She was in danger of being trapped. She was in danger of belonging.

Like it or not, the summer separation was bringing them closer together. My mother now understood Gísli's sentimental affection for the country in a way that she hadn't before, not entirely. It was about the light on the land, the way it both brightened and sharpened the mountain cliffs, and never faded them. And Gísli, for his part, was forced to accept her connection with the life of the country as a whole, and that she was now attached. They were less different than they had been when they met.

Only once during the seven years of their affair did they go out as a couple. It was on one of his first visits, when Gísli came over with an idea for dinner.

'Do you like otox?' he asked as he walked in.

'Otox? What is otox?'

'You know, otox. The sausage in the bread.'

'Do you mean hot dogs?'

He adjusted his lips.

'That's what I said, Susan. Otox. We have very good otox in Iceland.'

Mum hesitated as she collected her things.

'Well?' he asked.

'Maybe I should tell you: it's my birthday today. I'm thirty.'

'In Iceland,' he said, 'we do not have birthdays at home. I insist that we to go out to celebrate.'

It was one thing to be foreign, but even that didn't excuse my mother's plan to celebrate at home. A big birthday and not including all your friends . . . it bordered on the perverse. So, instead of picking up otox by the harbour, they went to Naustið, a Viking-boat-shaped restaurant downtown.

For Gísli, it was a brave moment; even the tourist traps were a dangerous place for a man with a secret, especially in a town where you always bumped into someone you knew. But that night, if only that night, he put aside his anxiety of discovery and took Mum out for dinner. He could, it seems, be that most southern and least Nordic of things, a gentleman.

My mother has a small list of moments when he did what open lovers do often. There was a gift, an opal ring that he gave her and that was later stolen in a transit lounge on one of our journeys back to Australia. There was a conversation when he confided in her about his money problems and his ambitions for his firm. Once, he even told her about his children and what they hoped for—his oldest daughter was an artist who was already winning her first commissions. They were islands of light in the otherwise shadowy, other life of his first family.

It was all a mistake, but then not all mistakes are bad. Auden, to prove the point, had meant it to be poets, not ports, when he wrote, 'the ports have names for the sea'. When he saw the proofs, though, he recognised the improvement, and left it as ports. My mother and Gísli were the same: their lives were better now than before they met. And that feeling is always going to be a difficult one to give up.

4

PAPER RUN

As I said, my mother's thirtieth birthday was unusual, and Gísli never again allowed himself to be seen in public with either her or me. He did, however, visit us in private as soon as we got back from Sydney in 1979, when Mum's old bosses had written to her to come back to Iceland.

'You must be Kári,' he said when I opened the door.

'Yes, I am.'

'I'm Gísli. I've come to see your mother. I wanted to see how she is.'

I let him in. This was the first time I had seen him; in the early years he had only visited when I was asleep. I had never even seen a photograph, but straight away I knew who he was. What did I recognise? A fatherly presence, his likeness to me? I'm not sure, but I understood what was happening.

He and Mum talked for a while in the lounge room. He was tall with fine brown hair. Then, from his wallet he drew a cheque for Mum and some *krónur* for me. I thanked him and ran across the street for a 7UP. When I came back, he was gone.

'Can I go get another one?' I asked.

'Is there enough left for another one?' Mum said.

'Yes. Look.'

'Well, of course, then. It's yours. Spend it on something you enjoy.'

And that was that. Mum said that she'd never wanted any money from him, but even Gísli must have noticed the relief in her eyes that night. I saw it, and I hoped he'd come again. I was overwhelmingly happy—to have him in our lives, to have a 7UP, and to see Mum not worrying about us. Mum told me that he had even promised that he would come to see us more often. But, of course, he didn't.

I can't help but think that he visited merely to reaffirm the promise, and to check that my mother hadn't changed during the two years we'd spent in Sydney. Once he learnt that she was still prepared to shelter him, he left. If I wanted to see him, I would have to find him for myself.

I was eight, and you could cut ice tunnels out of the banks of snow that piled up at the side of our street. My school, Álftamýri skóli, or 'Swan's Marsh School', was sited on a fairly harmless looking slope. When it was covered in lava ash we couldn't stay out too long. Without the ash, the ice made a wonderful slide that we couldn't be made to leave. The younger grades didn't start school until one, and so the mornings were ours to make all the tunnels or icy slides we wanted. The cold brought other pleasures, too. After a swim, we worked our hair into spikes, darts that snap froze in the morning air and could be broken off. The braver of us would hold our tongues against frozen windows to test whether it was true, as our parents had told us, that your tongue would stick to the glass and snap off.

'C'mon,' said my best friend at school, Óskar, 'try it.'

I did, and I slipped and fell down the stairs, banging my nose. The doctors said I would be okay. Then they poked, hooked and fished, and out came two abscesses, one out of each nostril, each deep green and about the size of a marble. Somehow, they didn't notice that I'd also broken my nose.

Downtown, we again ignored the warnings and cut across the pond, Tjörnin, which froze over during the coldest weeks. Ads running on TV taught you how to crawl over to someone who'd fallen through.

'What would you do if you fell in?' asked Óskar.

'I would stand up,' I replied. 'The water's only up to my waist.'

This was a cruel thing to say to Óskar, who was also only up to my waist. He would have to swim until I crawled over to save him.

I had small friends. Mum and I lived a little way out of town, and some miles from my school, in the suburb of Hraunbær, or 'Lava Farm'. My best friend there, Harri, was also at a dangerous height for falling through the ice. My new bike was much too big for him.

'Let me try it,' he begged.

'No, Harri, you're too small.'

'Kári, you can't have it to yourself.'

51

'But I only just got it.' Guðmundur, one of my mother's bosses at T & J, had bought it for me.

'It'll be fine. I promise.'

He got to the first corner, fell off, and smashed it. And himself. There was much hooking and prodding, and abscesses were found and extracted. The bike was put away and never repaired.

Óskar and Harri were doubles and I undertook all the standard misbehaviours of the day with both of them. We made peashooters by taking the fingers off plastic gloves and attaching them to plastic tubes. We chased busses, pretending we wanted to get on. We rang doorbells over and over, and set fire to polystyrene foam that lay on the unguarded worksites of Hraunbær. The lies I told were to them not the same, though. For the benefit of Óskar and my friends at school, I invented a father whose wealth was as great as his absence. He was an international businessman with his own jet, dividing his time between England and Iceland, dropping in now and then to ride in his Cadillac through the shabby streets of Reykjavík.

'Why are you here, then?' asked Óskar.

'He and Mum have separated,' I explained.

'Doesn't he give you any money?'

'Not really. But he would if we asked for it.'

Harri, who lived in the block adjacent to ours, was spared this elaborate invention. Probably, I couldn't see it working so close to home. Besides, he and I had just become workmates. There was a limit to the type of lies that you told a colleague.

When I rang Mum at T & J with the news of my new position, she said, 'What do you mean you have a job?'

'Hannes came around today and asked if anyone wanted to help with the gardening.'

'Gardening? What gardening?' Mum, who already felt bad about leaving me at home alone in the mornings, was seized by fear. But this was Iceland.

'In the block, of course,' I explained.

'Kári, you're much too young to work. Don't the older boys want to do it?'

'They don't think the pay is good enough.' It was the standard Icelandic response during the boom years.

'When does it start?' she asked.

'Now. It's okay, Mum. I'm bringing in a little extra money.'

It wasn't as bad as it sounds. Children had always worked in the summer months, normally back in the villages of their parents' childhoods, and the Reykjavík Council wanted to continue the tradition in town. As in the old days, we worked unsupervised—that was part of the nostalgic ideal, that children were free. In the evenings, my mother would hear us screaming, and take a panicky look from the balcony. I was usually pushing 'little Harri', as she called him, up and down the grass in a wheelbarrow. It was independence, the Icelandic dream, and it both amused and disturbed her. She was already seen as something of an ogre for insisting I came home before midnight. How could she stop me from working if I really wanted to?

When the gardening job came to an end, she had little choice but to let me join the line outside the offices of one of the daily papers. There were two, *Morgunblaðið* and its rival *Dagblaðið og Vísir*. Just about everyone had *Morgunblaðið* delivered, but not so much the other. It became my paper, and each day I joined the small army of nine, ten and eleven year olds who left the newspaper's distribution offices and marched past Hlemmur, the box-shaped bus terminal at the top of Laugavegur, and split up to cover the downtown streets.

This is how you sold a newspaper. You screamed '*Dagblaðiðogvísir*', as a single word and with all the stress on the 'Dag' and 'v', the others virtually unsounded. I was good at it. By my second day on the job, I was a double-satchel boy. I took Hverfisgata, a street of interminable roadworks, cheap apartments and rundown shops, and followed it along to the harbourside Vesturgata. This brought me into Vestubær proper, the old part of town.

'Dagblaðiðogvísir.' And sure enough a man would soon emerge out of his apartment.

'*Hérna vinur*,' he would say. ('Here, my friend.') Then I would turn up the hill towards Landakot, where the fancy offices were. There was nothing wrong with opening a door.

'Dagblaðiðogvísir.'

'*Já! Komdu.*' ('Yes! Come here.')

The money was wonderful and I was feeling full of independence. I think that must be why I decided to visit Gísli.

For some time, I had been aware that the paper run gave me an excuse to pop in and sell him a paper. What could be more natural than that? Gísli and his best friends, Margeir and Ragnar, were well established in their business as hardware importers in competition with the Black & Decker firm for which they'd once worked. Mum must have pointed out their office to me, because I found it straight away and opened the door.

'How can I help, dear?' asked the receptionist.

'Dagblaðiðogvísir.'

'Yes, we can hear you, friend,' she said. 'I don't need the paper, thank you.'

'What about in there?' I said, pointing at the door to the offices.

'Go in if you want,' she replied. Gísli and Ragnar were inside, sitting in facing rooms.

'Would you like a paper?' I asked.

'Hello, Kári,' said Gísli from his desk.

'Is it Kári?' called Ragnar. He too had worked with Mum at T & J and had known us as long as Gísli had. He came out to join us. I wish I could remember the look they exchanged, but all my attention was on my father. Was it as obvious to Ragnar as Gísli had always feared? He must have guessed. And perhaps that is why he would be the first person I ever told, just before the time Gísli and I met when I was seventeen, when he drove me to the president's lodge.

'How are you?' asked Gísli. He didn't show any discomfort. 'You're selling newspapers now.'

'Yes. Would you like to buy one?'

'We have ours delivered,' he said. He stroked my hair. 'How is your mother?'

'She's good.'

'You'll send her my best, won't you?'

'Yes,' I said.

'I'll buy one,' said Ragnar. 'It won't hurt to have two copies.'

'Thank you for dropping by,' said Gísli.

He didn't visit us again, and I couldn't call into his office after this. I took his not buying a newspaper to mean that he didn't want to see me. I wondered if I was being oversensitive but Mum didn't think so. For the first and only time I can remember, she was angry with Gísli.

'He couldn't even buy a lousy newspaper.' She called him a 'rotten bugger', the worst expletive I ever heard her say.

Mum was getting worried about me.

'You're just like your father,' she would say. She meant it as an ironic sort of compliment, an irrefutable declaration of disposition. 'You always want the most expensive things,' she would add, as final proof.

Once, the item under dispute was a bouncy ball and, this being Iceland in the early 1980s, the range wasn't great. The choice was between a cheap one and an expensive one, and of course I had chosen the expensive one. Yes, she had a point. I worked a lot because I liked to spend: bouncy balls, Matchbox cars, Lego. This, according to Mum, was a problem both cultural and genealogical.

'Your father always has to have the dearest of everything. Typical Icelander.' I took this to mean that he would have chosen the expensive bouncy ball, too.

According to Mum, I was becoming Icelandic in the following ways: showy and vain, materialistic, inquisitive, creative, and much too fond of Iceland, which, she conceded, was a problem that she and I shared. I was English, or a Diggons, or a Harold, in the following, single way: restless, like her. I could probably never be still, and I would probably never be satisfied, she'd said.

Where the countries and the two family trees met was in my independent spirit. Mum recognised it as the combined inheritance of two lost souls, hers and Gísli's, and she worried that I was heading the same way. I would go off for walks on my own. Usually I followed the bus routes around town, which I knew well, as Mum had never owned or driven a car since the Kombi van of her Ed years. But once I wanted to walk to visit Mum's friend Molly, and this was a problem as she lived on the other side of the river that ran along Hraunbær.

'I'll take you there if you like,' replied Mum. She didn't want me crossing the icy bridge on my own.

'No, Mum, please. I'm sure I'll be fine.'

'Let me call Molly.' She picked up the phone and, while she began to negotiate the terms of my visit, I got ready. This took a bit of doing: the boots, the inside pants under the outside pants, the jacket and gloves, scarf and hood.

'All right,' Mum said to me, eventually. 'Walk up on your own. But you're not to leave the path or go anywhere near the edge of the river.'

The day was grey and the snow seemed to merge with the sky above. I was aware of myself as a solitary blue suit against the whiteness. I was standing out clear in the world. Only solitude gave you that clarity. At the bridge, I stopped to look at the frozen edge of the stream. The ice was solid at the banks but became less translucent as it neared the thin line of moving water in the middle. There was a jumpable section there.

I tested the edge. It was firm. I could hear the stream

gurgling underneath, but I thought it would take my weight. I took my first step. A light strain appeared on the surface of the ice.

'I know you're there,' it seemed to say.

With my second step I was exposed. A crack. I bounced back.

'You made it,' said Molly when I arrived, 'and all by your-self, too.'

'Yes, it's not that far,' I replied. 'The river's frozen. Mum was worried I'd fall in.'

Testing the ice, I think, was how I celebrated my victory in being allowed to go across on my own. But more recently I learnt that Mum and Molly had worked out their own system for seeing me across safely. They were on the phone the whole time, with my mother watching until I got to the bridge, and Molly taking over the surveillance once I'd crossed. They were giving me something I loved, a sense of being solitary. But they were also keeping an eye on me.

For my part, I felt released by walking alone, as though solitude was an answer. I wasn't pretending when I was with others—I liked people and wanted to be with them as often as I could. My teachers in Iceland, as in Sydney, suffered because I wouldn't sit still. But even then I recognised that only solitude was real, and that this was because my social self was distanced from my inner life. I was aware that secrecy was a type of lying as well as a style of living. There was no such thing as a right to silence. But there was, I thought, a right to go off walking on my own.

I did this a lot, sometimes conspicuously, leaving school or after-school care and always following the bus routes home. I can't say that I spent my time alone thinking about Gísli, but I knew that the pleasure of walking was related to him, and that it somehow released the pressure of the fact that I was never not thinking about him. I knew that I had half-brothers and half-sisters, and that they knew nothing about me. I knew that these were their streets, too.

To most others, my mother and I seemed adrift. Her friends worried about us and invited us stay for Christmas and other holidays. Our doctor was worried, too. I was looking pale; Mum had to take me away so I could get some sun for a fortnight. So we joined the July exodus to Slovenia, where we were adopted by Gunnar and Lilja, an elderly, adrift couple who, like us, had been moved from the main, over-booked hotel to a quieter one down the road.

They broke a sacred tradition among Icelanders abroad by not being big drinkers, and by comparison seemed quiet and shy. At first, there was even a touch of embarrassment about the four of us being put together at a rather lonely table at the hotel restaurant.

'So you like sitting with us?' I asked on the second night.

'Thank you, Kári, we're fine here,' replied Lilja.

'Let them be,' whispered Mum.

'Do you like it here?' I called out.

'Yes, very much,' said Gunnar.

'What have you been doing?'

'Same as you, I expect. Relaxing, walking, having ice-cream. It's been so hot!'

'Where are you from?' I asked.

'Reykjavík. You are too, aren't you?'

'How do you know?'

'I heard you mentioning certain streets that I know.'

'I'm sorry,' interrupted Mum. 'Kári, let them have their dinner.'

'It's alright,' said Gunnar. 'But wouldn't you rather be left to yourselves?'

'Us?' said Mum. 'No, not at all.'

We had possibly found the only people in the world who were more concerned not to cause any trouble than we were.

'Do you go fishing much, Kári?' asked Gunnar.

'No, I've never been fishing.'

'That's good to hear. Fishing is the worst job in the world. There is very little enjoyment in it, and you must never let anyone talk you into it. I know, because I have a little boat called *Svanur*. In the summers, Lilja sends me out to catch haddock for her to put away in the freezer for winter. She won't let me back into harbour until I've caught a hundred, at least. Isn't that right, Lilja?'

'No, of course that's not right.'

'Don't listen to her, Kári. It has to be a hundred or I don't get my coffee. And no cigars. She has space in the freezer for a hundred, so a hundred it is. All for a cup of coffee.'

Coffee, I discovered on my first visit to their place later that year, was everything. It was late summer, and I'd been invited to drop in for pancakes. Gunnar and Lilja sat opposite each other at the kitchen table and slurped their black coffee through a sugar cube held between their teeth. When they were finished, Gunnar showed me around the house while he trailed lines of cigar smoke behind him. Whenever I could, I drew in deep breaths of it. I thought it was the most beautiful aroma I had ever smelt.

'When are we going fishing then, Kári?' he asked. 'I have to get these haddock in before the autumn.'

'I don't know, Gunnar. When does Lilja want you to go?'

'She says I should go tomorrow. But that would be too soon for you.'

'I'm free tomorrow.'

'All right, then. Let's go down to the harbour now and put *Svanur* in. Then, she'll be all ready for the morning.'

His red Lada spoke to the world from all its parts. They were separate in a way that I thought a car shouldn't be separate.

'This is a very fine car,' said Gunnar. 'A lot of people make fun of my Lada. Never listen to them, Kári. This is a good, honest car.'

'But it rattles.'

'Yes, and what do you think a car should do, dear Kári?'

'It should be smooth.'

'No, there you are mistaken. A car should always let you know what it's made of and what it's doing. Otherwise what's the point of all those bits and pieces? I paid for them. I might as well hear them.'

Mum and I had recently seen Gísli driving though town in his new car, which Mum somehow knew was the only one of its kind in Iceland. It had hummed past with an almost invisible quietness; even in the rain it was quiet. And here was Gunnar telling me that it was better for a car to be heard.

There was already someone else at the boat yard when we arrived.

'*Blessaður Gummi minn,*' said Gunnar. ('Bless you, my dear Gummi.')

'*Blessaður og sæll Gunnar. Hvað segir menn?*' came Gummi's reply. ('Bless you and greetings, Gunnar. What's news?')

'It's time to catch something, isn't it?' said Gunnar.

'*Svanur*'s day at last.'

'Yes. And, finally, I have some help.'

'How old are you?' asked Gummi.

'Nearly ten,' I replied.

'He looks pretty big for his age, Gunnar, but watch he doesn't get pulled in.'

'I promised his mother I'd bring him home.'

'One of your grandsons?'

'He is a friend, this one. We found him in Porta Rosa in the summer. But let's hope he fishes like a grandson. Let's hope he's a fishy one.'

The tug was tiny, as much a caricature of a boat as the real thing, and only just big enough for the two of us. When Gunnar put me at the helm, he was left to crouch in the cabin or move to the bow. This wasn't much fun, either way, as the smell of the engine invaded the cabin, and there was only a thin gangway to manoeuvre along the side of the boat before you got to the front.

It was calm out on the waters, but cold. I wore one of Lilja's *lopapeysa*, the fishermen's jumpers with coarse patterns chained across the chest. The others she sold to the souvenir shops or the knitter's cooperative. When we stopped, Gunnar set up four reels, each one with five hooks.

'We might as well bait them,' he said, 'even though we don't really need to. The fish probably won't know the difference.

Wait till you feel the line hit the bottom, then tug a little and wait for bites. When the line is heavy, draw it in.'

It wasn't a complicated business. A few minutes after I'd sunk the line, I drew in five fish.

'There we are, five meals already,' said Gunnar. He gave me a knife and showed me how to cut open the gullets. Then, we dropped the haddock into two holding frames wedged into the red floor of the boat.

'I hope we don't catch them too quickly,' I said. 'I don't want to go back yet.'

'I'm sure our luck will change eventually.'

I had gone looking for my father, and by accident I'd found Gunnar and Lilja. It was a good trade—even at the time, I could tell that. They were kind and warm, and never once saw either Mum or me as scandalous, a nuisance or, worse still, as the victims of my father's distance. Instead, they declared my mother to be another daughter and me a grandson. It was an adoption that we could accept, because it had no bearing on either my father or the secret of his identity, or at least not yet. One day, Gunnar and Lilja would play a part in that, too.

5

THE ARMY OF FOREIGN SECRETARIES

My mother's family was in England and Australia, and in some ways we were very much on our own. Mum told me that she didn't really get much help from her friends in Iceland, not practical help anyway. But in my memory of those early days, the other ex-pat secretaries were a constant presence, and they became a family of sorts for me. And just like any family, they openly disagreed with my mother's choices. Through them, I encountered an alternative to her forbearance. The Army of Foreign Secretaries wanted him to pay.

Everyone in the ex-pat circle could do a hundred-words-per-minute shorthand or efficiently transcribe from the Dictaphone. And as they had all moved to Iceland, they were necessarily a little mad. Maybe that's why I loved them so much. They had resigned their fate to whatever it was that drew them to the country. All the single women, apparently, were running away from something. There always seemed to be a secret, and the task for the others in the group was to work out what it was. An inability to define home, it was agreed, was often a cause of discontent. Also, broken engagements that had happened many years before but had left the victim unable to love again. United by fitting in where they least expected it, most of them had never felt at home anywhere else.

Nanci, big and loud and American, had once played hopscotch with famous jazz musicians and eventually met a man large enough to match her childhood. Haukur was a reporter who had come to Chicago for his degree in economics. He smoked four packets of Camel a day, and drank a bottle of vodka. But Nanci was the one who always seemed terminally ill, even long after Haukur, by then financial correspondent for the daily paper *Dagblaðið*, died, leaving behind him debts and promissory notes that her friends would never quite forgive him for.

Then there was Patricia, an Australian who lived in an attic flat that belonged to the glamorous Rut and her husband Bergur. Bigger and louder than even Nanci, Patricia drove her red Beetle each day to the American base at Keflavík, where she worked—and where she could obtain the ultimate luxury in Iceland, beer, which, like television on Thursdays, was banned until 1986. She was the part-time artist in the group, and her paintings and craftworks excited occasional admiration but mostly dread. Unsold at exhibitions, portraits of her numerous cats and dogs eventually became Christmas gifts, and were given discreet walls on which to hang.

English Judith moved in with Gestur, a younger man who was said to have the biggest collection of Elvis records in the country. One sensed that this made Gestur desirable, but Judith nervous. One corner of their apartment was devoted to a magnificent, black hi-fi system and so many shelves of The King that it would take a lifetime commitment to work through. But they remained unmarried—it didn't do to jinx such a delicate situation with legal obligations.

And Molly, with mysterious connections in the Channel Islands, had an aircraft engineer whose name was Steini and a summerhouse in Borgarfjörður, part of the wide bay that my mother had crossed in fog. There, in the afternoons, she stood on a narrow, homemade porch and called out to the birds while Steini stayed inside, smoked his pipe, and read through his back issues of *Private Eye* magazine. Steini, it was whispered, couldn't stand to fly, and so it was left to Molly to use up their quota of cheap international flights while he stayed at home and smoked his pipe. Her journeys, reportedly made for the cheap shopping in Glasgow, seemed always to involve stopovers in Jersey.

Nanci, Judith, Patricia, and Molly. They seemed to me at the core of my mother's group of ex-pat friends, although to her I know there were others, like Lilla, who left Iceland before I really got to know them. In the early days, before I was born and they became mine as much as Mum's, they met mainly to drink; first the beer from the American base but, as the night wore on, even less forgiving local drinks would do. This meant Black Death Vodka and Brennivin. The local custom was always observed: bottles once opened were emptied. It was a merciless system but it helped attract locals, or a particular kind of local. From what my mother has told me, it was usually the ones who ought to have been abroad. Theirs was an internal dislocation within Iceland that, paradoxically, became a match for the connection that the ex-pats felt. They understood why my mother and her friends had left their countries and, because they were as sentimental as all other Icelanders, they understood what you fell for when you came here.

Yes, this was a special country, the locals conceded: a community of only two hundred thousand people; an isolated and busy social world; a light that poets came to see. But what bemused and, to some extent, amused them was the way the foreign secretaries saw Iceland as a place for women. They claimed that it was a liberating country, and less sexist. On this point, the foreigners were surely mistaken—if ever a population of women had suffered, it was Icelandic women.

In the apartment below Patricia's, lived Rut, a shy beauty who spent most of the night putting up with or giggling at her husband, Bergur. Many years on, they would become two of my dearest friends and, just as in 1971 when my mother first met them, Bergur's humour would always run along a well-worn track. It was one Rut rather liked, a line of jokes that maintained that he was in fact the much-humbled victim of Rut's rule. Plenty of others would have liked that role, but as Bergur put it, 'It is awful being married to a beautiful woman. The beauty becomes oppressive. I have often tried to escape.' His modest line of work also was a source of great contention between them.

'I sell a few tyres,' he said with a look of resignation.

'Bergur!' said Rut, raising her eyes. 'Everybody knows you don't sell a few tyres.'

'What would you call it, dear?'

'I would say that you are rich.'

Give or take, that was the group I call the Icelandic Army of Foreign Secretaries. They had a campaign. For years they would insist that my mother reveal all about my parentage, and in doing so they only helped to fortify her position. They gave her a constant weight against which to put her shoulder, a steady focus for her resistance.

There was also one other member of their group, whose quietness was much more persuasive and might well have undone Mum's secret if they had each stayed in the country longer. Her name was Sóley, and she and my Mum left Iceland in their own ways. I believe they met some time after the army first formed, through my kindergarten. They were both single mothers, both with boys, and they fell into the habit of walking some of the way home together. Over the course of a year, they became friends, and perhaps because of the intensity of their situations, they formed a very deep bond. Sóley was even more dislocated within Iceland than the other local girls, and she was a quiet one, like Mum. Of the group, she was perhaps the most grounded, but also the most vulnerable, because she was the only other one with a child. While the rest became occasional parents to me, Sóley, during the short years we knew her, was more like an aunt.

＊

For Gísli, the Army of Foreign Secretaries could only have been a concern. He worried relentlessly that Ólöf, his wife, would find out about the affair. My mother told him that she would never tell them, but this didn't seem to help him much.

He couldn't but think that at one of the parties they held, an Icelandic girl might find out and, once an Icelander knew, all Icelanders would know.

Nervous but restless, and wanting more than his family life, Gísli would come and go. In this he was no different from Mum's restless father or Ed, whose adventures had taken him away to Antarctica and then to someone else. Perhaps, my mother reflected, that was how men were—wanderers and womanisers who now and then persuaded you that they were better than that. Or that they, at least, wanted to be better. She thought it would be preferable if they were simply honest and acknowledged their limitations.

At least partly as a result of a generally sympathetic attitude towards men, she accepted Gísli for who he was. In this she was quite different from her friends, who complained relentlessly about their boyfriends and husbands, and men in general. Mum never asked him to leave Ólöf. In fact, she dreaded the thought, and she would quietly practise her response were he to do so: she would escape to England. When she discovered she was pregnant with me, she had come to the conclusion that her main problem would not be him. Gísli, she told herself, was just Gísli—just a man. Money would be the real issue.

After years of living in Australia and England, where Scandinavian attitudes to sex were laughed at, she had come to accept that pregnant women couldn't stay on at work, and that a single woman with a child was even a little despised, and certainly not welcomed in the offices of a respectable firm. She thought she would be asked to leave at the end of her two-year contract on the grounds of moral unsuitability. It was impossible for her to know how Garðar, the less frightening of the two partners, would respond to her news. In the year and a half since she'd been there, he'd been reserved in the way of all Icelandic men, unless they were either tipsy or smitten. When she asked him for time off for a doctor's appointment, he replied, 'Yes, of course,' without asking why or when she'd be going.

The doctor didn't perform a pregnancy test—apparently, it was that obvious. He even seemed pleased for her, and certainly didn't understand her nervousness, or why she kept asking him if he was sure. It was hard for my mother to share in the celebration, but she didn't ask about abortion or adoption. This was all happening for a reason she'd figured, even if she wasn't sure what that reason was. She would keep the baby and take her chances with Garðar. Gísli, she decided, she would tell another day.

My mum knew Gísli was not like many Icelandic men. While it can't be claimed that Icelandic men are more involved in their children's lives than in other cultures, there is a strong sentiment in the community that a new child is a good event no matter the circumstances, a leftover from harsher times, perhaps. Even in the 1970s, the disgrace around illegitimacy that existed in other countries was barely present in Iceland, and children were seldom seen as interfering. Partly, this was because in most cases they were left to their own devices. Like everyone else in Iceland, children were expected to be independent. My mother had noticed the freedom of the local children with some concern, interpreting it, as most foreigners do, as neglect. She now feels it was a natural outcome of real affection.

It works, at least in a small community; but the unusual combination of warmth and self-reliance that permeated the culture was noticeably missing in Gísli. There is no way of putting this nicely: he was, in fact, the opposite in both—rather cold and strangely needy. He wanted Mum in his life as much as he wanted a large family, but he was capable of cutting Mum off at the first sign of trouble. And trouble had come.

Gísli simply wrote down his blood group and told my mother again of the utmost need for secrecy. He then added that he couldn't permit himself to see her again. He was, he said, out of her life. A month later he had left T & J and started his own firm. It would be a year before he visited her again and met me, his son, for the first time.

Garðar, on the other hand, couldn't have been any less surprised by the news.

'Oh, yes,' he'd said, 'I assumed you were pregnant when you told me you were seeing a doctor.'

She then waited for him to ask her to leave the company, but he just continued on with his work. My mother wondered whether he was completely heartless, making her stand there like that, contemplating her fate.

'Is there anything else, dear?' he eventually asked.

'But, Garðar, my job?'

'What do you mean? Do you want to leave?'

'No. I mean, can I keep working now that I'm pregnant? Would you prefer it if I left?' Garðar put down his pen and looked up at his foreign secretary.

'My dear, this is Iceland. We like children here. You can work for us as long as you want. I'm naturally very happy for you, and we're very happy with you. I think the staff would rather talk to you than to Guðmundur or to me. They think we are grumpy, you know.'

She wanted to cry, and she would have leant across the desk to kiss him, but he had already put his head down and returned to his work.

It was a conversation that was repeated almost word for word when she spoke to her landlord, Brynjólfur, about whether she would be able to stay in her apartment in Sólvallagata.

'What do you mean?' he said.

'Now that I'm having a baby.'

'What did you think we'd do, dear? Kick you out?'

That's exactly what she'd thought. She couldn't quite believe that a child could be so welcomed.

The Army of Foreign Secretaries weren't so sure about the situation. They were childless women living far from home, and they feared what was involved. There had been suspicions and signs, and for a little while talk of a romance that my mother was keeping to herself. Patricia, the most militant in the group, had tried to elicit some information. What was he like, this mystery man? What had drawn her to him? All she got in reply was, 'Well, I was lonely and he was clean.'

In the absence of something useful from my mother,

Patricia could always add her own view. It was something along the lines of not expecting much more than that from a man. And, in any case, no-one was shocked that my mother wasn't telling. And nor were they entirely disappointed. A mystery of this kind was just what the group needed; it was the type of business they were most expert at handling.

'Just be glad it's happening here,' added Patricia. 'There are good laws in Iceland.'

On either side of a long, wooden coffee table, the army of secretaries, foreign and local, smoked and nodded.

'You can get the bastard. I'll get him for you if you want,' Nanci growled.

Judith cast her nervous eyes across to the others and tapped her cigarette over the ashtray.

'What it means, Susan, is that he has to do his share. The law's quite clear. It doesn't matter whether you're married or not. He's up for his share.'

In this way, they announced from the very start that a war of sorts had begun. It would be fought on two fronts—against the father, which was easy; and against the mother, who wasn't anywhere near angry enough and needed mobilising.

'But what are you going to do?' Judith persisted.

'Oh, have a baby, I suppose,' Mum replied.

'Aren't you worried?'

'Of course, I'm terrified. I haven't got a clue what to do with a baby.'

The group nodded their agreement to this. Having a baby looked hard. All the same, they weren't fools. They knew this was the beginning of one of my mother's evasions. They tried again at dinner. She would at least have to confront the father, even if she wouldn't tell them who he was. This reticence—or, even worse, politeness or delicacy—wouldn't do.

Bergur tapped a fork on his glass.

'May I speak?' he said.

He was the only man in the room. The army, less willing than usual to indulge him, ignored his tapping. Bergur stood up.

'May I please speak?' he repeated.

'What can you have to say about this?' asked Patricia.

'A great deal,' replied Bergur. 'I have a great deal to say about this. And other things.'

'Stop it, Bergur,' Rut tried.

'I have gotten up,' he said, 'to tell you all something very important.'

The room fell silent.

'I am standing up here tonight to declare to you all that I, Bergur Jónsson, tyre merchant and property holder, am the father of Susan's child.'

Rut grabbed Bergur's arm and dragged him back into his seat.

'Sit down, you stupid man!' she cried.

But the table applauded, and once again the evening bent away from its main topic, and its mission to unearth the secret man and set my mother against him. They interpreted his ongoing absence as you only could: the father was married and, hopefully not as Bergur had declared, one of their husbands. My mother smiled back at the curiosity of her friends, desperately glad that they had stopped asking. She would again and again refuse to tell them what they wanted to know and, really, needed to not know. Not knowing was more fun. But naturally, from then on, every man she was seen with was added to the list of suspects.

They had no idea, and never did work it out for themselves.

6

LEAVING ICELAND

My mother didn't want to be a mystery. Like most real mysteries, she just wanted to be left alone. In writing this book, I am merely the latest in a long line-up of friends and relatives who've sought to understand the overlap of her peculiar combination of qualities: shyness, generosity, and restlessness. They all somehow found a home in her treatment of my father, but also in the very intense bond that developed between her and me, especially during our early years in Iceland, when our sense of his absence still defined what we shared, rather than how we differed.

The truth is that, like all stories, this one has its limitations. Stories make grand claims about helping us order and understand the past and, yet, so often all they really do is create a sense of order around puzzles that will survive all the literary treatment you can throw at them. Just when I am ready to discover a reason for this or that, real life reimposes its uncertainties, and I am left with guesses. Actually, I haven't done much besides lay a claim to *a* truth about my mother. But my guess about her motives is better than hers: I believe she was in love with Gísli, even though she has always said that love had very little to do with it.

The point, of course, is that one day I hoped to take a different path from the one my mother had chosen. We had our own individual reasons for thinking the way we did about Gísli. She eventually tired of him, while at the same time she promised to protect him. I hoped to find him, and eventually be open about who he was to me. I couldn't give up on my father. I think my mother always understood this about me and was waiting for the day I took a different approach to hers.

To others it might have seemed a contradiction, but my mother thought she could work out a way of being honest and secretive at the same time. True, it was a difficult combination, and virtually impossible in Iceland, where it was always assumed that everyone should be known, and that all things were knowable. But it was how she reconciled herself to her new world, one in which she felt at once proud of me and guilty about Gísli. The combination comes through most clearly in the story she tells about my birth, and how the government forms, which were all about the appearance of openness, forced a kind of deceit that was to haunt me for years.

◢

It was mid September, 1972. After months of total light, a short night announced the arrival of autumn. The first really cold snap arrived, marking the beginning of my mother's second winter in Iceland. At around ten in the evening, when the day ended over the south-western shore, green pulses of light arrived, each one as urgent as those seen the year before. They were the northern lights, which called people back from their holidays abroad or their time on the farms, and heralded the time when tourists left and the most exquisite time of year began.

In the three months leading up to Christmas, life in Iceland becomes more internal, moving from the fields and parks to the concrete, earthquake-proof homes; from the social and unexpected to the private and familiar. It is also a busy time. Children spend their days behind triple-glazed windows at school, while their parents take on extra jobs to keep up with money problems.

My mother was heavily pregnant, and Patricia was worried that she wasn't getting enough help. The problem with Susan, Patricia said, was that she kept everything too close to her chest—that was her way. Patricia insisted Mum come and stay at her place for the last few days. Mum could have the spare room, eat Australian food, and they could begin the final wait together. It was the least she could do as a fellow Australian.

So my mother moved in to Patricia's attic apartment above Bergur and Rut's. The following Friday evening, there was a knock on her door.

'I'm Ed,' said a bearded man on the doorstep. 'Brun-jul-pur said I'd find her here.'

'Who? Who did he say you'd find?'

'Susan Reid. My wife.'

'Wait here.' Patricia closed the door. She wasn't going to let a man in just because he claimed to be Susan's husband. She walked inside and looked at Mum and said, 'Ed?'

'Ed? Really?' Mum replied.

'Yes. Your husband, apparently.'

'Yes, my husband.' Mum began lifting herself off the couch but it was a slow and cumbersome process. 'Sorry, Patricia.'

'You stay there,' Patricia said, looking back to the door. 'I'd better get him, then.' When she returned with Ed, she pointed to Susan and declared, 'You can squeeze on the couch in between us.'

'You look fabulous,' said Ed. 'I bought you these.' He reached over to his duty-free shopping bag and extracted a box of chocolates that were too big for Mum to hold, so he took them back to hold them for her.

After a while Mum announced they were going to stay in her flat in Sólvallagata. She couldn't impose the two of them on Patricia. There were protests from Patricia but none from Ed, who understood that he had entered a hostile environment.

'No, I'm calling a taxi,' insisted Susan, asking Ed to fetch the phone.

On the way back to my mother's apartment, Ed explained that he was glad to be in Iceland: he'd been reading *Njál's Saga*.

'Well,' replied Mum, 'you'll be glad to know that I'm going to call the baby Kári if it's a boy.'

'After Kári the avenger,' said Ed.

'I'm not sure what he does. I got the idea for the name from Patricia's landlords. They called their son Kári.'

'It's Kári who takes revenge for the deaths of Njál and his family. Kári kills all of the burners and then reconciles with the leader Flosi.'

Ed had his Penguin Classics copy of the saga at the top of

his pack and that night, as my mother's contractions began, he pulled it out to read to her, to show her just who Kári was. He would leave his copy with her after he left, and she'd have it on her bookshelves until I finally discovered the saga when I was eighteen, after returning from my meeting with Gísli.

The following morning, my mother was squeezed with her box of chocolates into the doctor's car and they sped through the arched streets of the Valla area. When they arrived at the hospital the midwife ushered my Mum towards the lift, looking quizzically at the chocolates.

'Am I supposed to carry these?'

'My husband gave them to me,' Mum said. 'He said I should bring them.'

'What do these men think? You'll have to help me hold them. I've got a form to fill in.' The midwife rested the chocolates half on her own arm and half against Mum's side and, with her free hand, she began to fill out the admissions form. It was awkward, but she wanted to make a start on the paperwork before they arrived at the ward.

'Husband's name?' she asked.

'Edwin Reid.'

'Edvin Raid,' she said. 'Have I spelt it right?' My mother looked down at the form.

'Yes.' And there it was.

Mum hadn't meant it to happen, but that was how Ed had been given as my father, and when she woke up after the birth and scanned the forms by her bed, she saw that not only was the real father hidden, but that he was hidden by her ex-husband.

Ed was rather pleased with all this. Like Bergur before him, he would be happy to see his name on the forms. There were now two men who wanted to be my father, while the real one couldn't even manage the sight of my mother. And, then, there came a third. Gísli's brother, Pétur, added himself to the line of those offering their names for the forms. But Mum refused. What was the point in lying? All she wanted was to be allowed to not say who the father was.

Was silence such an unbearable thing? In Iceland, yes. Icelanders had been keeping close records since settlement eleven hundred years before, and they weren't about to give up now. They demanded completeness from Susan Reid—she was foreign, yes, but she was having her child in Iceland and she needed to play her part in the national project of tracing the connections between all Icelanders of all time. The minute relations between everyone, living or dead, were the essence of what it meant to live here.

The patronymic system, which produced a second name out of your father's first, was and still is alive in Iceland. The patronym is formed by adding son or daughter's name to the genitive form of the father's first name, with the result that each generation has a different second name. I ought to have been called Kári Gíslason—Gísla being the genitive of Gísli. Instead, I was given Ed's surname, as Mum had kept her married name. Indeed, the two hadn't yet legally divorced.

She was told priests could correct birth certificates, and she found one who was prepared to leave blank the space in the 'father's name' column. As it turned out, the law was ahead of her and her futile attempts at silence. It said that, in the absence of a declaration of fatherhood, the mother's husband was deemed to be the father. So, even though the first physical copy of my birth certificate was made enigmatic by a kindly cleric, by law I was deemed to be Ed's child—the reprints of my birth certificate contained the addendum. I was Kári Reid.

Sometimes I'm asked what I think about what happened at that point, when I was born and the father's name was first called for. The question assumes that my mum was at a defining point in her relationship with Gísli. I think my mother would reply that she hadn't seen him since she'd fallen pregnant, and had no reason to think that he'd ever come back into our lives. Where was the gain for either her or me in naming a married man as my father? I think she just wanted to get on with being a mother.

Even without a local scandal, this wasn't going to be easy: she had only five weeks' maternity leave before she returned to full-time work at T & J. At the time she lived in a basement apartment that felt even more confined than usual in the approaching winter months with a baby to care for. Her parents in Australia were not the sort to visit, and her friends in Iceland were somehow missing the point about her. Why add Gísli to all this? There was, after all, a hidden danger in revealing him as the father: she could end up with him.

No, it was better to be alone.

A few weeks after my birth Ed left, chasing news that his girlfriend was now in England and ready to be pursued again.

He left behind him a dozen sketches of Iceland and scenes that he recreated from *Njál's Saga*. My mother covered the walls of the apartment with them and, from then on, his fine sketches accompanied us around the world, in each place forming a link to our basement studio in Reykjavík, as well as a roving exhibition of the work. Ed disappeared from our lives and we wouldn't see him again until I was a young man at university, reading his copy of the saga he'd brought with him to Iceland.

My mother hadn't wanted Ed back, but neither was it easy to see him leave once more. She was alone again, just as she had been when Ed had left the marriage three years earlier. Gísli still hadn't come to see us, and nor did she think he ever would. She detected a new distance when she made her phone calls to her father in Australia. He seemed to find a border to erect between them. This, then, was what it meant to have a child: you gave yourself completely over to the child, while everyone else ran away. She'd never really known what she wanted from the men in her life, but it couldn't have been this. And so she let Gísli back in when he came around, as free of obligations to her as when they'd first met.

Gísli had been in love with my mother, as he had confessed to me seventeen years later. After I was born and he realised she wasn't going to name him, he began to relax a little and started visiting Mum again. We spent the first five years of my life in Reykjavík, and for all of that time I didn't once see Gísli. He worried that I might recognise him in the street. But he visited Sólvallagata in the evenings, after I'd gone to sleep. Mum says that he liked to stand over my bed, talking to me while I slept. That was the extent of our early contact.

He wasn't an unfeeling father, I am sure of that. But from the very beginning, our resemblance terrified him. And you have to concede that it was a cruel irony for him to have produced his double in this way. But to have denied himself the sight of his child looking at him is a bewildering thought to me. My two sons are both under five, the age I was when the affair between Mum and Gísli ended, and I can't imagine that I could ever have been as disciplined as he was. I would have woken the boys, or at least made one visit before bedtime. But such is the disgrace of an affair, isn't it? He was betraying his other children, and he made a choice about how to protect them from the truth.

By the time of my fifth birthday, Mum had had enough. She says it was just going on and on. He wasn't going to leave his family and, in a way, I think she admired him for it. He had a sense of loyalty, even if it was a conflicted one. And every time she asked herself the testing question—what would she do if he left his wife?—her answer was always the same: I'd run a mile.

I've often wondered why. Can it be that, after seven years, she didn't want him to herself, and that she feared rather than hoped that he might leave Ólöf? I think so. I'm not going to disagree with my mother on this one, because seven years would be enough time to spend in the company of his fears, even if you were in love. He wanted closeness and distance combined, intimacy and borders—for Mum and me to be nearby, but for no-one to know—and this left her with very little. In the end, the only way to stop it properly was to move back to Australia, to Sydney, and the shark net at Balmoral.

She had not become bitter through the experience of living in Iceland, because she had come to believe the Icelandic position on parenthood, which is that it was always a gain. And she has always refused to see herself as a victim of men in general, or Gísli in particular. It was her choice, she says. She didn't want Gísli's help. Being a single parent in Iceland wasn't all that bad. But I have often wondered whether that was true, especially when I think about Sóley, my mother's friend who was also a single mum.

They became close because they both struggled as a result of the men in their lives, but Mum thought Sóley's position much worse than hers. Sóley, she'd said, didn't have any contact with the father of her child. She was a local girl that everyone had known before she fell pregnant, the father a foreigner. The father was black, and Iceland was still racist. Sóley was worried about money even more than my mother was. All this made it harder for her to cope. I am not in a position to judge as I can't really ever know what Sóley and my mother went through, or how self-reliant they were. But I often return to questions about their lives back then because Sóley, the only person who understood my mother properly and deeply, took her own life when her son was very young.

My mother was grief-stricken. But she was also angry, and I suspect that is because my mother understood the temptation. I remember that Mum sometimes spoke about a long swim she would have liked to take, out beyond the current of her worries in life. What exactly those worries were, I was never sure, and even now I find that I'm still guessing. Money, yes, I understood that. But, as a child, I sensed that money problems veiled a more acute pain, one that was tied to the knowledge that there was no help coming, and never would be. Gísli was a lost cause, and she had a line to maintain: that she didn't want his help, anyway.

Despite the talk of a long swim, she was never going to leave me, of that she was sure. Instead, we went on our swims together at the big pool at Laugardalslaug, near the Reykjavík camp ground. Some days, we would walk down to the pool during her lunch break—it meant meeting in her office facing Mount Esja, and crunching along the ash-covered snow towards the sea and a valley of hot springs where the modern pool had been built. She would swim a leisurely breaststroke, while my aim was always to sprint ahead towards the deep end, where the water was cooler. But we were inseparable. For the first time in her life, she had someone who depended on her, someone who wasn't needing to leave.

When it came time to leave Iceland, the Army of Foreign Secretaries, never convinced by my mother's assertion of independence, wished her well in the pursuit of a rich new husband and predicted that, like all Icelanders, I would one day be back. When that time came, they would surely have another chance to solve the mystery of who my father was.

7

WIRRAL RATS

In 1982, three years after we'd moved back to Reykjavík from Sydney, we moved yet again. In a way, it was another step back, to her birthplace and the home comforts she imagined in Oxford. But, in retrospect, I wonder whether it wasn't just England's turn again. After all, we'd tried Iceland twice, and Sydney. There was still something missing, indistinct but quite possible just over the horizon, too. I was ten now, and becoming more aware of the true nature of our situation, and indeed Mum's character. But, all the same, on a British Rail train trip I bought coffee for a stranger and, returning to my seat, told Mum that he would have to buy her one now. However mysterious my mother's search might have been, mine remained a transparent one.

Sales representatives who visited T & J from England had assured Mum that she would pick up work easily if she returned to her birthplace. But when we arrived, we found the country was heading into recession and, for the first time in her life, my mother couldn't find a job. Anyone, it seemed, could be a secretary these days. The IBM golf ball just about typed your letters for you. Bosses were surprised when you told them you had shorthand, as though it were an anachronism to have such a useful skill. So she moved from one temp job to the next while we stayed in B & Bs, with old friends or with Mildred's family in Yorkshire. It was hopeless. We had lost Iceland, and what for? The damp life of English itinerants; Iceland without the wind and the social support.

Then, my mother had an idea.

'Would you like a trip to Australia?' she asked me. She suggested I could go and live with my Aunty Lee, Mum's sister.

'On my own?'

'Luv, I can't keep moving you around like this. You need to go to school. Be settled. And it'll only be for six weeks or so. I'll have more time to look and have a better chance of finding work. As soon as I've got a permanent job, I'll send for you.'

I was the same age as Mum was when the Diggons family had first moved to Thumb Creek. If I was looking for patterns and cycles, I would say that it seemed the right age for a solo trip. While Mum's had been on Bluey, mine was on a Singapore Airlines 747. My travelling companions were a troop of light-footed hostesses in tight dresses who moved me every three or four hours—to the cockpit for a chat with the pilots, to an empty bar on the top deck for a sleep, and up to one of the wide, first-class seats for the landing. Like Mum's ride on Bluey, the flight confirmed a twin loss, ones I suppose we all face at some point in our lives: your parents have to let you go, and you have to leave home.

My Thumb Creek was the village of Cowwarr in Gippsland,

Victoria, a dry, expansive region of farms and mills. There was a small school, not unlike Thumb Creek, with Mr Morcom, a kindly teacher in shorts, long socks, and a brown, short-sleeved shirt.

'We have a new student, today,' he said when I arrived for my first day. 'He's come from a long way away, from Iceland in fact.' The others looked at me, each with the open faces of bush kids.

'I think we should welcome him with a geography quiz. We'll expect you to win this one, Kári. Take out a clean sheet of paper . . .'

We did.

'. . . and write down all the countries you can think of.'

Just as at Thumb Creek School, my welcome was given the same exotic spin that Mum's had had, in my case it was formed out of a list of twenty-two countries of the world. After class, the other kids crowded me in, asked about Iceland, and offered me visits to their farms. The McCredie boys were insistent. They were the animal collectors of the class. They would show me their snakes, and possums, and lizards, and guns. They would let me drive an old car they'd been given. The McCredies, along with my cousin Ray, also wanted to show me round the back of the shop. This was because it was the one place in Cowwarr you weren't allowed to go.

'It's full of snakes back there,' said Aunty Lee. But buried in the long grass was a great treasure, the wreck of a white Ford Falcon. It had wide seats and a big steering wheel, soft-worn pedals, and crunching gears.

'Have you ever seen a snake in here?' I asked Ray.

'Lots.'

'Are they dangerous?'

'Yep.'

'Could they kill you?'

'Yep.'

The McCredies said they'd keep an eye out for us as they wanted to catch a snake.

'Do you really think you'd be able to catch one if you saw it?' I asked.

'Yep.'

Cowwarr was that sort of town. A 'Yep' town.

I'm sure I seemed strange to them. When Aunty Lee took my cousins and me shopping in Traralgon, the nearest big town, I spent fourteen of my fifteen-dollar allowance for the special outing on a red, Parker 45 fountain pen. It's the defining story of my personality, Aunty Lee had said, and she tells it every time we meet.

'Can you imagine,' she always says, 'a ten year old spending all his money on a fountain pen.'

Like many small towns, Cowwarr had picked a moment in history that it liked and stuck with it. It would always be the late fifties there, and this came as a shock to someone from Iceland, where everyone dealt with their sentimentality by rushing at the future. Aunty Lee and her husband Lindsay wore the hairstyles of the film heroes from their youth, and the friends who came through their screen door at the back invariably had their ciggies rolled into the sleeves of their shirts and took up a leaning position against the wall. It was the James Dean lean, I now realise. If there wasn't a wall handy, they put their feet up on a stool and leant forward against their knees.

'Do you like Elvis?' Aunty Lee asked me.

'Yes, I've heard a lot of Elvis songs. One of Mum's friends has the biggest Elvis collection in Iceland.'

'That must be quite something,' said Lindsay. 'The biggest collection in Iceland! But what about The Beatles, Kári? Lee's nuts about them.'

'Oh yes, they're okay, too. But I really like Roger Whittaker and Engelbert Humperdinck.'

'Is that what they're listening to in Iceland?' asked Lindsay.

'Yes. But I'm not sure that Mum likes Engelbert Humperdinck as much as me.'

'Thank goodness for that,' said Lindsay.

'But she loves Roger Whittaker. She has two of his cassettes.'

'Dear me,' said Aunty Lee. 'The whistler?'

'Yes, that's him.' I whistled a few bars of 'Old Durham Town'. Even then, it was my kind of song, over-sentimental and all about a long-held regret over home. And it fitted Cowwarr better than Aunty Lee would have liked to admit. This village cared only for itself and the little scandals, heroics and comedies of rural life. I understood it all: the footy club, the pub, the corner shop—they were the Australian versions of the smallness I cherished in Iceland. The plot points . . . this time I saw them for what they were.

I stayed at Cowwarr for three months, and then there came news from Mum that she'd found a permanent job at last. It was hard to leave. Melbourne Airport was treated to the Diggons' side of the family as they embraced in a rare moment of raw family emotion.

'You poor thing,' said the hostess. 'You'll see your Mum and Dad again soon, won't you?'

'Yes,' I replied. 'I'm flying to Mum now.'

The hostess gave me a sideways look. I didn't understand why I was so upset at leaving Aunty Lee and Uncle Lindsay, and I was too distressed to think about why going home suddenly seemed as difficult as it was when I left it. But perhaps I had begun to realise that home would never again be an automatic thought, and that instead it would always flicker like a broken light between Iceland, England, and Australia.

My mother met me off the plane and we went to a B & B.

'I'll be working at a school,' she told me. 'You'll get to go there. It's a boarding school called "Mostyn House". You'll be sleeping in a dorm with the other boys. You won't mind that too much, will you?'

Yes, I would. I think I'd reached my limit. We had left Iceland, I had been sent on my own to Australia, and now I was losing my mother again. I threw myself under the phone table and cried, and for the rest of the evening clung to Mum's legs, imploring her to call the school and say no to the job. She couldn't, of course, but by the end of the night she offered as much. She'd call the whole thing off if I really wanted her to. But, she asked, what would she do instead?

Here was another echo of Mum's early life, how she had cried to Harold after her first day at Thumb Creek School, a signature story for their relationship. For a year, my half-day

Sunday visits home always ended with me crying my way back along the bleak, long corridor of the back entrance to the school, which we used after home visits. Other boys, many younger than me, didn't see their parents at all during term; perhaps that would have been easier than these Sunday partings. But I was one of the weak ones, or dramatic ones, or lost ones, and the weekly separations were awful.

Strangely, they also made me less independent than I'd been in Iceland. My early friendships at the school formed quickly and became intense, needy even. I would look out for my mother whenever I passed her office and when I knew she would be on her way home after work. I thought more and more about Gísli and where he might be. And out of those thoughts I began to imagine a life that I thought he ought to have.

Apart from the Sunday visits home, there was nothing for us beyond the school gates, and any mingling with kids from the nearby state school was punished with detention. The school, rather like Iceland, saw itself as an island apart. A young teacher who had just come down from Oxford, himself an ex-pupil, yelled at us for ten minutes for talking over the fence to the 'local fucking scum'. But, then, most signs of humanity were punished here: no hands in pockets, no dragging your feet, no talking, no eating, and so on. It was all standard boarding school stuff. Your entire world mediated through rules, conditions and, eventually, privileges—a total institution as the theorist Foucault called it. Even the depth of your evening bath was marked by a dot, and we 'first' and 'second' bathers were timed to the minute.

Food, like hot water, was served up by monitors with the portions entirely at their discretion, and often painfully unfair. In the mornings, the unpopular boys woke to find their clothes smeared in Vaseline. On other nights, their beds were up-ended in a ritual known as the 'lamppost'. The idea was to trap the victim at the base of his upturned bed. The only way out was for him to push the bed down off the wall, which would wake Matron and bring her up from a lair she occupied somewhere near Blue Dorm.

It never paid to disturb a Matron, and this one was no different. Called 'Wooden Tit' because of her rumoured replacement breast, she had an unpredictable smack that expressed all her frustrations sharply and without pity. You'd hear, 'Don't eat like a monkey', just seconds before she hit you on the back of your head. Once, when Griffiths spilt his milk and took a blow from Matron, Wilson said to him, 'Don't cry over spilt milk.' He was trying to be funny to appease Griffiths, but Wilson shouldn't have said anything; he was, after all, one of the boys routinely lampposted. Griffiths picked up a steel serving spoon.

'I'm going to kill you, Wilson,' he yelled. Matron tried to calm him.

'Get away from me, you stupid fucking bitch,' he replied. 'Get the fuck away from me.' Matron held out her hand, and he hit it. 'Get away from me, you one-tit cow.'

It was wonderful, and dreadful. And that was how it went. No-one got angry until they were ready to go completely mad. It wasn't worth it otherwise, because only the moments of total despair went unpunished. There was always some sympathy for the ones who lost it in the way Griffiths did that night.

I was sitting next to him and I knew, and felt precisely, everything his anger expressed: a dozen lousy farewells, weeks of homesickness, and the nagging sense that we were here because our parents wanted us out of the way. Then, when Matron hit you on the back of the head, you exploded. I had never liked Griffiths much, but after that night I liked him very much. I wanted one of his explosions for myself.

For me, it came in the television room. I had a front-row seat and it was Thursday night, *Top of the Pops* night, easily the most important night of the week. The room was filling up as more and more boys came in. Owen stood in front of me and said, 'monitor's privilege'. I had to move back a row to let him have the seat. Then, Durant stood in front of me and said, 'monitor's privilege'. I looked behind and the room was now full, and I had to stand.

'No,' I replied.

'Get the fuck out of the seat, Reid,' he said.

'Get fucked,' I replied.

'Get to the back, scum,' he insisted.

I dived for him, and punched him in the hipbone, while I buried my head in his stomach. He fell over the end of the bench, and the two of us hit the wall together. He was unsettled, panicked, and he was waiting for me to finish it. It was my chance. I might kill him. I dragged myself towards his face. Hit him, I thought. And, then, for a moment at least, I stopped thinking altogether. I was at him, and he wasn't fighting back.

Mrs Billington, my biology teacher, stepped in.

'Get up! Get up!' she shouted. 'You know the rule,' she said. 'Outside.' I walked out of the television room and began watching the programme from the window.

'Not there, either,' Billington yelled. 'No TV if you fight.'

All these unnatural rules couldn't have been more removed from the freedoms I'd had in Reykjavík and Australia. But rules produced order and rhythm, and it was a productive school—I was never idle. Rules also produced those unexpected releases, when the energy beneath became too much to contain. It seemed as though nothing would happen, but then suddenly there was an escape. The structures collapsed as the TV room became an untidy fight scene, and the insanity of order was revealed.

Not that I thought such things then. No. Later that night, I merely worried that Durant would get back at me somehow, and that I wouldn't be up to much in our second round. I knew that, without anger, I was a pushover. But he didn't come for me. Instead, the next time we met, he looked ashamed, as though I'd beaten him, when all I'd really done is fall on him.

I was no hero, no match for my namesake from *Njál's Saga*. The creed of the Vikings was to act coldly—only cowards needed anger as a fuel for action. More fitting prototypes lay further south. Like Hamlet, I waited until the last minute, reflecting endlessly on my absent father until fate drew an action out of me. Or, like Odysseus, wandering from island to island, seemingly avoiding home instead of looking for it.

Mostyn House School was where you learnt to put up with life: as in all total institutions, a great deal of our energy went into naturalising the conditions of our imprisonment, and making it seem as though nothing would change. It was self-consciously a school of systems and, of course, the first system it taught you was to get along without your parents.

Yet there was a paradox. Despite all of the school's structures, its approach to knowledge and, in particular, language was free and wonderfully encouraging. It was thanks to Mostyn House that I eventually went to university, I'm sure. I was the first person on my mother's side of the family to do so. At the age of ten, I could only read and write in Icelandic but the school gave me English, my mother's tongue.

I was put into 'Non-Latin', the charming name given to remedial English classes that ran at the same time as Latin was put on for the rest of the school. A dozen of us spent an hour with Miss King and her fountain pen. She was, in fact, all about pens, as I had once been myself and would eventually become again. She was a great corrector. But it took someone like Mr Boston, who taught me geography, to later recognise my abilities and intellect, and that was because I was an oddity, his favourite type in life.

Mr Boston was pleased that I was from Iceland and that I'd flown directly from Australia to attend the school. It meant he could defer to me on topics as wide-ranging as marsupials, volcanoes, cod stocks, Vikings, QANTAS and the Fischer-Spassky game, which, he told me, was held in Reykjavík on the year of my birth.

'It was the match of the century,' he said, 'as I'm sure you know.' As a matter of fact, I did. But what pleased Mr Boston even more than my complex origins was my even hand, my grace with the pen, and here he was probably indebted to Miss

King and her early insistence on the proper shaping of letters. The exercise books that I left in the school desks at the far corner of the New Wing were, he said, exemplary. I had the neatest handwriting in the school, the least complex, and I was barely two years in.

It was not the most sought-after honour in the school, but it would have to do. I was tall, big for my age, as Mum had been as a child, and that was enough to get me picked for most of the sports teams. But I was only ever competent, never fast or clean with the ball. Yet, when it came to handwriting, no-one doubted my skills, and for three years running I claimed the little-known Mostyn House School Handwriting Cup.

I now see that my handwriting influenced the way I wrote, and what I had to say. But also the way I read. It was the shape of language on paper that mattered as much to me as meaning. Perhaps because my understanding was imperfect, I found English more visual than Icelandic, as though English were really a language of symbols and shapes, not words. It outlined the world rather than saying it directly—a language of suggestion rather than expression. Why else have so many words that no-one understands properly? And, most pleasant of all, English even took you away from meaning towards a hazy oblivion, rather like my fight with Durant. The language was textured, but it was also blank. You went at it, and it kind of disappeared. Take the metaphorical way Mr Grenfell, the Headmaster, spoke to us.

Every school morning began with an Anglican service: a psalm, a hymn, a reading, and that most English of touches, the daily announcement—normally a birthday or an achievement, but quite often a problem. And, often, the announcement contained two of Mr Grenfell's phrases that I couldn't ever fully naturalise: he was 'sick to the back teeth', and our behaviour 'stuck out like a sore thumb'. Was he being literal? Could one look at his back teeth? Was there at some point a sore thumb sticking out?

But I fell in love with English, and with the hours you could spend inside it, as though you were entering a series of rooms, each one taking you further from your original intention, each one a brush stroke separated from the final painting. It didn't matter whether you understood what all the words meant, or, at least, I didn't think so. What mattered was that there was an alternative to the Mostyn House grind, to the clarity and the precision of the school system, and it was an alternative that the school, to its credit, sponsored in very rich English classes. In its attitude to the language, the school had in fact found an extra room, a second self that was full of imagination and feeling. I became the English student, the one who loved the set texts and whose stories were read out to class. At the same time, I forgot every word of Icelandic I'd ever known.

English was so indecisive, confusing and obscene even. In the end of year play, I performed the part of the Vicar of a small village. I had the line, 'warm the cockles of my heart'. To my surprise, a hammy delivery of this line drew a laugh. I had no idea why but I came to think that there must have been some sexual innuendo attached to cockles, and that a cock was involved. How there came to be a penis of the heart, I didn't understand at all.

There were other confusions. Exotic and erotic meant quite

different things. This became clear during Mr Grenfell's much-anticipated 'chat about sex'.

'Boys,' he said. 'The way I usually do this is through an exercise.' We looked at each other unsure of what he meant.

'It's a word exercise,' he went on. 'What I would like ...' and he'd paused on like, 'is for us as a group ...' and he'd paused on group, 'to come up with a list of nicknames for ...' and he'd paused one last time before he said, '... condom.'

A dozen hands went up.

'Yes, Durant.'

'French letter, sir.'

'Good. Yes, French letter is one. Wilkinson.'

'Sir, Johnny.'

'Excellent. Yes, you Leroy.'

'Rubber, sir.'

'Yes, Rubber. American I think. But that's okay. Shaw, you're next.'

'Raincoat, sir.'

'Really?'

'Yes. Raincoat in the shower, sir.'

'Well. All right then. Thank you, Shaw.'

'Prophylactic.'

'Who was that?' asked Grenfell.

'Me, sir, Wilson.'

'Not really a nickname, wouldn't you say?'

'No, sir, not really.'

And on it went until there was no doubt in our subtle English minds that the best thing to do during moments of Continental intimacy was to wear a Johnny, a rubber, and raincoat, even if Mr Grenfell had never quite said so. It was another moment of humanity in a school that understood itself through rules, when what he gave us in place of precision and instruction was the suggestion of things, and words with the merest imprint of real life on them. Imprecision meant that they had their own life. Sex was unclear, unstructured and, above all, the property of language.

Every morning for the next two weeks, blown-up and brightly-coloured condoms appeared in the library, the tea room, in hallways, and were tied to door handles. The school was overrun.

'Do you know where they're all coming from?' asked my mother. I didn't. 'Mr Grenfell thinks it's probably Durant.'

'Really, Mum, I don't know; honestly, they just appear.'

'He's quite distressed about it. He thinks it's aimed at him.'

I knew the school loved language, but I was never clear about how it regarded our stories, the narratives of how we'd all ended up at Mostyn House. I sensed that these were meant to go unsaid, or veiled by fiction and subtle, ironic references. As a boy living in Iceland, I had simply lied about my father, exaggerating what I knew and inventing details for what I didn't. Now, in England, I felt the rise of some non-fiction, the beginnings of a process that has now found its, perhaps final, expression in the story I am telling here. I wanted to speak about Gísli as plainly as I could, and I was always on the look-out for the friend or teacher who might be my first audience, or reader, if you like. In the end, it was Powell, whom I had only recently befriended—another one of my fast-forming, intense friendships—after my best friend West and I had fallen out over a pen he wanted to borrow.

Powell and I were standing on a low bench, and looking out over the window ledge. We could see the salty marsh of the Wirral and, beyond it, the mud-brown outline of Wales. It was dull, as always. There was not much life—just the occasional walker and, rarely, a rat scurrying across the marsh.

'My father lives in Iceland,' I told Powell.

'Yes, we know that. What does he do there?' he asked.

'He's a rich businessman.' And he really was.

'Are your parents divorced?'

'I haven't told anyone this before, but my mother and father weren't married when I was born. It was an affair. My father is married to another woman. And when I was born my mother was still married to her husband in Australia.'

'That's a shame,' he replied. There was a pause, and for a moment the strange solemnity of children confiding a secret.

'There's one,' Powell then said. 'A rat. Did you see it?'

This, then, was more important. James Herbert's *The Rats* was doing the rounds, shadowing the three copies of *The Lord of the Rings* that were slowly making their way through the school. The marsh rat outside was about the size of a cat, a shadowy, humped thing.

'Imagine if it got in,' said Powell. 'They could make it the fucking school mascot.' Were we really already onto a different topic? Was that it? Was this all it took to tell the truth? And what was the reaction? Kindly indifference.

'You don't care?' I asked.

'I couldn't give a fuck,' said Powell. 'Your mum's nice. Who cares about your dad? How often do you think I see my dad?'

He had a point. The other children might well have come from respectable homes, but few of them saw their parents as often as I saw my mother. Somewhere in the past, their parents had decided that it was better to have your children raised for you and, in the majority of cases, it had been discretionary—this was a very wealthy group. Whatever people say about taking responsibility for your own life, Mum's decisions were never entirely her own. She had been desperate when she took the job.

And Gísli, for all his nervousness, did not really choose how he behaved towards me. He was the flirt who had lost control of his life and had been unable to collect it back. He had fallen in love twice, when he thought he would only ever fall in love once. He had had another child, when he thought his family was big enough.

In Powell's mind, if not mine, there was nothing that could be done about any of it, about any of these things. There were tides. There were the rats inside, and a solitary, humped rat outside. Sooner or later, the tide would turn, and we would get out.

8

ON THE LÁKE

I made my first return to Iceland when I was twelve. I went on
my own during the school summer holidays at the invitation
of Gunnar and Lilja and, although only two years had passed
since we'd lived in Reykjavík, I was barely able to communi-
cate. I had even forgotten the Icelandic for toilet. This was a
problem, as I had just come off the plane and I was desperate. Gunnar and Lilja spoke no English. I remembered the verb
pissa but, after two years in an English boarding school, I was
all too aware of good manners to use it.

'What do you want, dear?' asked Lilja.

'Well,' said Gunnar, 'do you want to piss?'

Poor man, I can't imagine what was going through his
mind. I was about to spend the next month with them without a word of Icelandic. How were we going to cope without
language?

'It'll come back,' Gunnar said, hopefully.

The first thing we needed to do was to go fishing. It was
summer and time to bring in his hundred haddock, and *Svanur*

was already in the water, waiting. The next day we drove to the pebble shore in the Lada, which rattled less now, a sign that it was getting older, settling down. We steamed out of Reykjavík in the boat and Gunnar passed me the rudder and pointed in the direction of the deep, haddocky waters. Half an hour later, I was drawing up fish the length of my arm as the tug rocked evenly on the bay.

During the weekdays I helped out in Gunnar's shop in Vesturbær, mainly stacking bottles and staring whenever I could at Gunnar's granddaughter, Björk, who'd captivated me simply by the fact that she was female. I was twelve and she was eighteen, a woman. I could forgive the difference in our ages if only she would. I even knew a dozen or so English words for condom to impress her. I spent the whole week looking for excuses to come out from the bottle room, as Björk never came in. She was clearly meant for the checkout, she was that kind of girl. She had a perm that made her look beautiful, which, even at the time, seemed unusual.

For me, there was an alternative to Björk even if she didn't know it. If I had wanted to, I could have devoted myself to a higher being: the president. Vigdís Finnbogadóttir, who held office for sixteen years from the early 1980s, was a regular at the shop. Her home, where she stayed when she didn't need to be at the presidential lodge, was also in Vesturbær. Gunnar introduced me to her and suggested I help Vigdís with her shopping. I wheeled the trolley while she picked out items, making light conversation about life in an English boarding school as she did.

'Your Icelandic is coming back, though,' she said. 'I hope

you're going to come back to us one day, too. We wouldn't want you to forget your Icelandic all over again; and your good friends are here, too. Have you been to visit your old friends from school?'

I didn't really want to go into details, but Óskar and Harri had disappeared from my world. The friends I'd found had on my return, to my horror, remembered my lies about Gísli and his jet.

'It's hard, though,' I said, 'to pick up old friendships.'

'That should never be too hard, Kári,' said Vigdís, 'if they were good friends.'

'Harri and Óskar were my best friends. They've both moved.'

'But you have Gunnar and Lilja. They are surely the best kind of friends.'

'Yes, and that's their granddaughter, Björk.'

'Yes, I know her. She's lovely, isn't she.'

Gunnar made plans for us to visit his relations in Borgarfjörður, to help with making hay. I pretended to like the idea, even though it would mean a week away from Björk and her permed ringlets. Gunnar loaded the Lada and we left Reykjavík for the road going north along the base of Mount Esja and up and down Hvalsfjörður, or 'Whale Fjord'.

We stopped at the small town of Borgarnes, as everyone still does today even though there is a tunnel under Hvalsfjörður and you don't really need the break at that point. But Icelanders can only drive for so long without either an ice-cream or a hot dog, and the traffic seems to pull off almost automatically into the exit lane at any cluster of service stations and roadside cafés.

The farm was on the west coast and had hayfields that sloped down to the edge of the sea, and a shoreline of fading spits of black lava rock skirted by gold-brown seaweed. A standby workforce of half-a-dozen children in woollen jumpers and half-a-dozen Icelandic sheepdogs with contracted faces and upturned, bushy tails waited for its chance to work. I was given a spot in the line-up, along with boots, a pitchfork and a woollen jumper, and told to wait.

We were to follow the tractor into the field to collect hay at the base of each stack for the men to lift on to the tops. It was pleasant, repetitive work—like walking uphill, or swimming—and in every way possible removed from my school life in England, where even sport was treated with some distance and irony. I noticed the difference and liked it. However fragile a conception it may seem to me now, it was then that I felt Iceland could survive in me as the site of less-complicated, and more-instinctual rhythms.

It wasn't long before we children were allowed to climb to the top of the stacks. Instead of helping with the collection, we stood waiting for the hay to thump at our feet so that we could stomp on top of it, supposedly with the aim of compacting the hay but really just to have fun. The sun, as the poet Steinn Steinarr says, was 'like a thin girl in yellow shoes', and never more than that—a thin girl who stood beside you while you 'worked' and looked past the hayfields towards the sea.

When we returned, Björk had disappeared, invited to some ludicrous life outside the shop. Her absence took the pleasure out of being there, and so I went swimming. Gunnar and Lilja lived close to Laugardalur pool and Molly—of the army of secretaries—had bought me a ten-swim pass, which was hole-punched at a front counter made of security glass and high timber by a woman who paused her knitting just long enough to do so. Inside, I found that the change room was the same as it had been when I'd left two years before, a seemingly constant rampage of naked boys flicking each other with towels while screaming–singing English pop songs. There were also the two pale men dressed in white who did the job of making sure everyone washed properly, and then sprayed us with cold water to get us out of the shower.

The army, too, was unchanged in composition but for Mum, the only one to have left. I was to visit them all, and each one had asked me in turn what my favourite food was. Thereafter, whenever I visited or stayed with one of them I was served lamb chops. At Patricia's they came with her greying hair and much of the cats' hair, too. It was that sort of house.

I hadn't shaken my childish sleeping habit of using my toes to play with the buttons at the end of the bedcover, and Patricia's cats, delighted by this nocturnal movement, scratched at my feet all night. In the morning, I woke to find my toes lined with thin scabs and the sheet dotted with dried blood. I would then put my shoes on my bloodied feet and run outside to walk the dogs. Patricia, who had become larger and larger until she was barely able to walk, preferred to drive when she took her dogs for their daily walk, so I would run at the side of the car with them. In this manner, the four of us—two dogs, a boy, and the large Australian inside a small car—would edge our way to Highway 1 and back again.

Molly and Steini had moved from their house near the frozen river and into Vesturbær, not far from Gunnar's shop. Steini talked to me only in Icelandic, which made communication one-sided, but he was at least beginning to share his back volumes of *Private Eye*—apparently, I was old enough now. Molly talked only about her travels, which most often still took in a side-trip to Jersey. She showed me a card index of her friends around the world.

'I send every single one a Christmas card,' she said. She was up to 250 cards; the index was the only way she had to keep up with them all.

'I can stay with any of them whenever I want.'

Judith remembered that in the old days I had enjoyed lighting the girls' cigarettes. She dug around for a lighter she thought I should have. It whistled a dozen songs, including 'Are You Lonesome Tonight'.

'Doesn't Gestur want it?' I asked.

'I think he's got enough Elvis memorabilia by now,' she replied. Apparently, there was a limit to how desirable he could be.

Nanci was disgruntled I wasn't staying with her for at least a couple of nights. She made less-than-kind comments about Patricia's animal den because I had slept over there. Her own cats, said Nanci, would never be allowed the run of the house like that. And why would you have dogs?

'Australians love dogs,' I explained.

'My dear, so do Americans. But we don't keep them inside.'
I pondered this for a moment.

'In Australia, people have backyards, somewhere for the dogs to run.'

'Isn't that why dogs were banned in Reykjavík in the first place?' asked Nanci. 'They should at least be castrated.' Over our game of Yatzee, she added, 'Has Patricia talked to you about your father?'

'Patricia?'

'Yes. Has she mentioned anything to you?'

'She asked me whether I was contacting my Icelandic side.'

'I know you can't tell me who he is. But does Patricia know who he is?'

'I don't think so. I haven't told anyone,' I replied.

'Your mother might have told her. She and Patricia were very close in the old days. Both Australians.'

'Mum thinks of herself as English.'

'Well, same thing. At least your mother doesn't go in for dogs.'

'Or castrations.'

'Well, I suppose that wouldn't be such a bad thing.'

Each of my dinners with the army members had been accompanied by conversation along these lines, reminders that it was only a matter of time before I would have to tell. Or, tell them at least. They had given up on getting the information out of Mum, that much was certain. They knew she would never relent and, in any case, she was too far away to be worked on properly with booze, cigarettes, and an atmosphere of indulgent gossip. But I must have been showing signs of weakness. In my own mind, it wasn't a possibility; I would never let Mum down in that way. But I could see that they believed, that one day, I would switch allegiances and become part of their hunt for my father.

In 1985, as I entered my teens, old friends from Mum's days with Ed offered her a job in Brisbane.

'We'll have to go back via Iceland,' she said. 'It'll be my last trip there, I'm sure. A farewell.'

It would, at least, be the last time I visited before I met Gísli at the president's lodge.

'Why do you think you won't go again?' I asked.

'Well, I can't keep going backwards and forwards like this. I'm sure you'll get other chances. But it's time I settled down.'

Even today, I don't think she has accepted that she doesn't have a choice about Iceland. It won't let go of her, and returning to say farewell was her way of checking that Iceland was still there, more or less unchanged. There was no way of farewelling Iceland, only ways of going back.

On that trip, we stayed with Molly and Steini, and they took us for a week's stay at their summerhouse by a lake in Borgarfjörður. I was set up with a fishing rod and a dingy, which I took out onto the lake and towards a small, wooded island. The idea was to drag the line behind me as I rowed. Steini and I had tried it earlier while we motored, but each time I lifted a silver trout to the surface it escaped, a shining dart that flicked back under the thin surface of grey water. I didn't care much that we kept losing fish, but Steini became frustrated.

'As soon as he's on the line, hook him. A good yank at the right moment and he's yours.'

I couldn't get it, and blamed the speed of the boat. Under my own power, it would be different, I reasoned, and so I took off solo and rowed past the island to the more sheltered water on the far side of the lake. This channel opened onto a cove a little further along that caught my eye. I took the boat in, and found myself perfectly out of sight of the summerhouse. A light breeze passed through the heads. Now and again, it brought what I thought was Molly's cooing, or perhaps it was just cooing. Birds were all around me, and it could well have been them.

I didn't want to go back. I hadn't caught any fish, but I didn't care much about that, not now. The solitude in Iceland was still perfect and on that day only my paddling, which I could temper, broke it. Iceland had not been the site of personal catastrophe. There had been disasters of sorts in mine and my mother's lives, but the country itself had escaped unpolluted. It remained an island of simple, more elemental, life—walking and swimming, rowing, fishing, and haymaking. Although life here was simple, it also seemed to offer a more complete version of how to be. It didn't occur to me at the time, but I see it now, that I had begun to regard Iceland as the place I went to become more fully myself, just as my mother had done in the 1970s.

When I did eventually row back, I followed the shoreline

of birch trees and mossy grass, which sheltered me further and kept me out of sight until, at last, I emerged into the open stretch of shoreline in front of the summerhouse. On the balcony, I saw the three of them waving me in.

'You had us worried us sick,' Mum said when I got to the shore. It was about as close as she'd ever come to yelling at me.

'Why?' I asked.

'We couldn't see you. Whatever made you want to go out so far?'

I think I could have said that I liked the feeling of drifting out of sight, of solitude in the stretches of quiet water, just as much as she did.

9

THIN GIRLS IN YELLOW SHOES

There was, I felt, an alternative universe in Iceland, and it had something to do with love and nostalgia: my parents' affair, the light, and the unthinking rhythms of childhood. But in Brisbane, where we came to live in 1986, love seemed everywhere. Before I even realised it, the girls here were smiling at me. No reserve. No Icelandic sullenness. No English snobbishness. They were all thin and wore yellow shoes—or seemed to, such was the effect of the sun and the brilliance it produced when it met the skin.

Time passed as a series of failed crushes. Katrina, I was told, I had missed my chance with by a week—she was now taken. Kristeen was simply bemused by me. Jane said that I'd do as a formal partner but, no, she couldn't imagine anything beyond that. So it all came down to Nadia, the only girl at school who didn't seem taken by the yellow of the Australian sky, and who kept herself out of the sun and away from the outdoor life it sponsored. And that wasn't until 1989, when I was sixteen and in my last year of school in the outer Brisbane suburb of Brighton—a year before I met my father.

Nadia was small but strong, and had dyed her hair jet black. She had a backpack of badges: The Smiths, The Cure, The Mission, The Clash—you needed a definite article to get on. So maybe I would do for her; after all, I played guitar and wrote poetry. Nothing could dissuade me from these, not even my best friend Colin who said I was 'just a wanker'. I knew I was a complicated young man but Nadia was different too. She was fucked-up but not in a considered way; you just sensed that something was amiss. You weren't surprised when she told you that you were over-analysing her. But in fact her greatest appeal lay in those odd moments when she appeared to acknowledge the missing piece, the absence or sadness that drew you to her. It was a side that, now and then, she wanted someone else to see.

Colin—like me, tall and rather obnoxious in class—would check out what Nadia and her friend Janine were up to from behind the high taps of the biology classroom. He wasn't interested in Nadia, she wasn't his type, but then she wasn't exactly mine, either. I had always fallen for bright-eyed girls with big hair, like Katrina of the best legs in the history of legs, or the delicate, indifferent ones like Björk in Reykjavík. That is what I initially told Janine, Nadia's best friend, when she asked whether I'd go on a date with her. I'd said that Nadia and I weren't suited, 'she's into The Clash and The Mission'.

'How about we go out as a group—bring Colin and some others', suggested Janine. So that's why a group of ten of us met at Albert Street, outside the bottle shop at The Victory Hotel, on the night Nadia and I got together.

'Who's going to get the booze?' asked Melinda. Drinking

was considered *the* thing to do—Expo '88, for all it offered in terms of urban renewal, wasn't much good to underage drinkers.

'There's no point us going in,' replied Nadia. 'We look thirteen.'

So I collected the money and told the others to keep going towards the Botanical Gardens. Colin stood guard for me and, when I came out with only wine, he expressed his usual, unsubtle view of me; something like, 'I can't believe you only got wine, you wanker.'

We caught up with the others inside the garden gates.

'Where are we going to go now?' asked Colin.

'Let's drink it there,' Will, the sporty one in the group, said. 'Over on that bench. That'll do.' He then promptly sat on the backrest, propped up like a thin, metal figure.

We were underneath a fig tree, it was nine o'clock on a Saturday night, and there wasn't much else going on around us, just a rustle from the dark every now and then. A torchlight flashed on to us and the voice that went with it asked, 'Having a nice evening?' We told the police we were and they warned us to be careful in the gardens at night.

'You haven't seen any Aboriginal people, have you?' one asked.

'No, none,' I replied.

With that, they ignored the wine and left us in peace. We decided to catch a ferry across to Kangaroo Point. When we got across the river Janine led us past the back of the hospital and on to a cliff ledge. On the way, Nadia surprised me by holding my hand. A set of dark steps ran down to a house fronted with tall windows. It stood silent and empty but for the scattered belongings of past squatters and drunks.

'Nadia, how do you even know about this place?' Colin asked.

'Jesus, Colin,' said Janine. 'There's more to life than Brighton, you know.'

This was about as close as you got to the 'left bank' of Brisbane, and it was actually rather lovely. The Story Bridge was lit up on our right, and the skyrises of the city stood close to the water on the other side. It was warm and hazy, as it always was in this town, even in winter.

As the night wore on Will got drunker, Janine began to understand Colin's sarcasm, and Nadia's body got closer to mine, until we were almost touching sides. I wasn't used to this kind of sophisticated, out-of-the-way location for a booze-up. All the parties I'd been to before this one had led only to fights, vomity snogs, and long walks home. That was just the Brighton way.

Our night on the cliff face ended when the booze did. We dragged the drunk ones back up the steps, reboarded the ferry, and made the last train to Brighton. The ride back was fluorescent and revealing, in that way of all brightly lit public spaces. You became conscious of your zits and suburban taste in clothes. Nadia, though, forgave all this in me, and we held hands again as we made the slow midnight walk from the station to her home. It wasn't the same as falling in love, but I could feel something stirring all the same.

We only went on one date after that. She arrived in a white dress with pink polka dots, and wore black Doc Marten boots with yellow shoelaces—her gesture to the yellow shoes of the other girls and the sunshine that inhabited them. My response to her off-key beauty was to take her to an awful, local play about Brisbane nurses in the 1950s. We sat in the back row and kissed. I tried to get into a good position, but failed. I was too tall for the seats, which cramped my knees and pushed my legs sideways. So Nadia sat up, tossed her hair back, and leant in for a second kiss. It was a glorious, superior kiss. She was taller, over me, and in control. The audience disappeared.

That kiss . . . well, I nearly got over it by the end of the following year, after eighteen months of thinking about her commanding presence at the back of the theatre, and her hair as it enclosed me. Nadia got over it before the end of the night. She had something else on, and told me she would be fine to make her own way to the bus. She waved me goodbye from the lower end of the Queen Street Mall. Despite my following her home from school for the next three months, at a visible distance, she didn't seek out another one of those kisses.

It was the start of a trend for me. For the next ten years girls like Nadia, fucked-up but friendly, drew out of me a melancholic, needy side that I suspected of being Icelandic in origin, and probably had something to do with my father. They all shared Nadia's evasive style of only rarely acknowledging an inner disquiet, and I thought they wanted that to be acknowledged by me, as well. So I did it the only way I knew how—writing up to five incomprehensible poems a night. I fell in love more easily than I could write a single lucid sentence, and each day I swung between gregariousness and sullenness.

What was I looking for in a girl? Puzzles, I suppose, that were nice to be with. Enigmas like Mum? Perhaps that, too. Like her, the thin girls in yellow shoes would say, 'Never mind that' or 'You're not still thinking about that, are you?' I could never quite be light-hearted in the kind of way others were. They would denounce love and poetry, and insist that life was just the steady march of nothing-muches. But I was turning into a serious young man who knew better than they. And, perhaps unsurprisingly, it was about this time that my mother, sensing that I was perhaps a little too inclined to poetry, suggested I take the year off.

'Why go straight to university?' she asked. 'Spend some time in England, maybe visit Iceland. You could look up your father.'

Although she claimed to have stopped moving around herself, she hadn't yet stopped believing in the power of travel. I think she even saw it as her main gift to me—being restless was a virtue. I loved that about her, but my restlessness had different ends. She had always travelled as a way of feeling at home, and saw travel as an end in itself, while I travelled as a way of finding home. I was going back, not out into the greater world.

In ways that she didn't really want to discuss, Mum and I were still the same. Like her, I couldn't altogether separate Iceland from Gísli—he and the promise that surrounded him remained at the centre of an island community that I imagined was still mine. Finding home remained tied to finding him. And, even if I had never stopped to wonder why, I was sure that I loved him as much as I loved Iceland.

Jessica was not only the most beautiful girl in Aviemore in 1990; she also had the second-best working perm of all time. Since Björk, I had thought this more or less impossible. After all, that was 1984, and this was 1990. A lot had changed, including hairstyles, in those years.

I'd arrived in England in January to a winter of poll-tax riots and storms. I sheltered in a Westminster café with a Swiss girl in a bodysuit—I was not yet serious enough not to see this as wholly good. Outside the wind brought down trees; inside I fell in love and wrote my five poems for her. Then, I travelled to Nantwich and stayed with West, my best friend from Mostyn House School. We joked about how we had once fallen out over a pen, and for a second time made up, this time over beer in The Crown Hotel, a bar that tipped along the uneven lines of its Tudor frame.

'Where are you from?' asked the bar manager. When I replied Brisbane, he offered me a job. Mum had been right— you just went and got a job.

For the next two months I pulled pints. Then at Easter I wandered north to Aviemore in the Cairngorms with a letter of recommendation from a friend in the Glasgow Council. I arrived on a bright, spring morning, and sat in the sun watching the snow as it began to melt. The town was divided between modest streets of Highland housing and the Stakis resort, which stood a little apart from local life with its hotels and its large ice rink, go-kart track, and staff hostels.

There wasn't really any work going, the recruitment officer at the big hotel told me. 'But have a word with Andrew at The Rox, our nightclub. I think he needs a bouncer. You know, someone to stand at the door, collect glasses, break-up fights,' he added.

My experience in this area was obviously limited. I had been kicked in the balls by a certain Tommy when I nine, and I had fallen angrily on Durant when I was twelve. But my lack of know-how didn't seem to matter to Andrew.

'Show me your hands,' he said in his slow, unusually even Glaswegian. I held them out for him, flat out in front. No. He wanted me to lift them up.

'Yes, they should do.' I didn't understand what he meant.

'Here's the thing,' he said, 'this is a resort town. We don't hire big doormen. What we want is tall, thin men with big hands. If there's a fight, get in and pick up any glass you see left standing. Straight away. And try not to take on the locals. They've been wanting to close us down for years. Highland Presbyterians.'

Andrew was also tall and thin with big hands, and so was Jason, a Jordie and the head bouncer, as was Alex, another Glaswegian with a handsome, battered face who immediately told me he'd had seventeen assault convictions by the time he was thirty. The others were all the same: tall, thin, and violent.

'We had an Australian here, before,' Alex said. 'He was fine until he knocked up a local girl. Took off last month. You're the replacement.'

'Is it a very rough club?' I asked.

'The squadies from Dundee can be a handful,' said Jason. 'Just make sure you fuck them up before they fuck you up.'

'Right.' Clearly, I would need to toughen up.

'Who broke your nose?' he asked.

'Me.'

'Oh, Jesus. What have we got here, lads? A fucking Australian who breaks his own nose.'

'Well, I fell down some steps. In Iceland, actually.'

'Right.' He meant, shut up, and went on, 'Try not to hit a local. Try to look reasonably capable. You're working tonight. It's a rave. No booze, just water and pills. Shouldn't be any trouble at all. Smile, be nice.'

The rave was held in a nearby conference hall given over to a few, cheap blue lights and an end-of-room bar that sold only bottled water, at five pounds each. It was twelve hours of acid music, and I was bored senseless after the first hour. I walked up and down in a daze and then I tripped. What caught me? An outstretched leg. I could see it being drawn back. Be nice. Smile.

'Did you just trip me?' I asked the leg's owner, an enormous, broad man with smallish hands. They looked hard.

'Yes, I did.' He leaned forward and, with a heavy smile, growled, 'I was hit by a car this evening, and I've been on the beers since. Now, I want someone to fight.'

'Right.' I sounded weak. What to do next. Kick him out? That was unlikely. Hit him?

'And you're fucking English!' he continued.

'No, actually I'm not.'

'You're fucking English,' he said again, smiling.

'I'm Australian,' I told him, as I wondered whether he was the brother of the pregnant girl?

'Come here. C'mon.'

Fuck it, I thought. I was busting for something to happen. I dreaded the thought of having to hit someone but maybe this would be a defining moment. I might as well get it over with. So I moved in and then . . . he hugged me.

'I love Australians,' he said. 'Except for that bastard who just left.' He was yelling over the music, but the intention was friendly. 'Leave the local girls alone.'

'Sounds a good idea.'

'You don't want that nose broken again.'

'No.'

'We'll watch out for you.' A Highlands threat, I wondered.

That was the closest I came to a fight. The locals and the other bouncers soon learnt that I was either incapable of hitting someone or not prepared to try. Both were true. And, strangely, they liked this about me.

Jason and I became close. Like so many of my friends from this time on, and all of my girlfriends, he was inhabited by a sadness that he didn't understand, and which he mistakenly thought I might be able to articulate for him. Out of that sadness came an extraordinary punch, a deadly, short-arm jab that detonated as it made contact. He'd say to me, 'Come in with me,' keeping me close but out of harm's way, and then he'd hit one of the drunks, just once. The punches, or rather their sound, made me nauseous, but one hit was always enough to end it. Never before had I seen grown men run away like those before Jason, tripping over themselves to get out of his way. It was decisive, and so completely at odds with my own laboured complexity, that he engrossed me.

Alex didn't tower like Jason; he scuffled. He was a street fighter. He said he was only concerned with speed; unlike Jason, who was one-punch elegance and timing—something power gave you. He would drag me in to the scuffles and then hold me off—keep the boss happy by giving me some level of involvement, and then stop me from getting hurt.

The reason they protected me, and the reason we became friends, was that they were both romantics, and I sometimes suspected they wanted me to write poetry for them. Perhaps, wanting me to write poems about them.

In the early evenings before work, when we were allowed on to the ice rink, all eight of us bouncers would meet and skate together. The jukebox was unlocked, and for an hour we danced—invariably, it was U2's cover of 'Unchained Melody' that began and ended our sessions. The other bouncers made wonderful, elegant skaters—Jason, in particular. But every now and then, he would stop his jumps and quite deliberately smash into one of us. He couldn't manage an hour's exercise without violence of some kind.

One night, during a party at one of the staff hostels, Jessica appeared. She had just gotten a job at one of the hotel restaurants, and moved into the smaller of the hostels, across the main courtyard from my own. I was seventeen, she was twenty-three—but I looked older for my age.

'Where are you from?' I yelled above the music.

'Kirckaldy. You won't know it. Just a wee bit north of

Edinburgh.' The way she said the name of the town was wasp-ish, thin, and musical, just like her.

'That has to be the sexiest accent in the world,' I said.

'Very nice of you to say so.'

When she danced, she flicked her light perm in every direction, but mostly in mine. I fell in love, and wrote six incomprehensible poems. Isn't that what you do? Sometime during the weeks that followed, she asked me why I wrote so much.

'Can't you just live for the moment? Do you have to record everything?'

'Yes. But some things only make sense on paper.' As far as I was concerned, that was living for the moment.

'Things like us?'

'Not us, but you. You only make sense on paper. How else could I understand you? You're a poem, aren't you?'

'I'm sure I'm not the only one. You write a dozen a week, don't you?'

'You don't trust me?'

'Do you think I'm mad? I can tell a flirty guy when I meet one,' she said. The comment wasn't really fair as I was much too self-concerned to flirt.

'But I'm yours, entirely,' I told her.

'You'll be gone before I am.' For good measure, she added that this was who I was: the guy who was always on the verge of leaving. And yet she herself had run, from Edinburgh. Her boyfriend cheated on her and, she said, 'didn't even have the guts to admit it', when she found out about it. He was a coward, she'd said.

'He wasn't even a good liar. Even now, he won't admit it. Don't you think that's the worst thing you can do,' she asked me, 'cheat on someone you love?'

'No,' I replied. 'I think the worst thing is to leave the one you love.'

On one of the rare occasions that we had a day off work together, we hired a car and drove up to Ullapool, a village on the West Coast, for a break from the staff hostels and the heavy drinking in Aviemore. The village ran along a little fjord with a white beach and unlikely palm trees. During lunch, in one of the white pubs on the seaside road, I told her about Gísli, and that I would have to visit Iceland soon if I was going to make it there before I returned to Brisbane in December.

'What's the rush to go back?' she asked.

'University. I'm enrolled for next February—in literature.'

'Don't you like it here?'

'I adore it,' I replied. 'I think it's the friendliest, most beautiful place I've ever lived. Apart from Iceland, I mean. Iceland's less friendly, but more beautiful.'

'You'll go, I'm sure,' she replied. 'I could live here, in Ullapool. I could live here without even seeing it. What a name, Ullapool! And all you talk about is going.'

As Jessica drove back it was dark and quiet. She didn't want to talk, and I let my thoughts run ahead to Iceland. Nanci of the army of secretaries had agreed to have me stay for a month from mid August to mid September. Haukur was away getting treatment for his addictions, and she wanted the company. I would need to contact Gísli—I knew that. How could I go back and not, even if there had been no word from him, nothing to suggest that he wanted to see either me or Mum?

I wish I could remember more of what was going through my mind that night and during the week or so that I remained in Scotland. Some years ago, I gave away my journal for that year—an impetuous gift to another girl who I thought ought to read my poetry. But that night, I must have realised that my love life was beginning to clash with my attachment to Iceland, and perhaps I foresaw that this, too, was the start of a trend. Jessica was pulling away, and it was because I was leaving. And yet I couldn't cancel my trip to Iceland, not now that it was so close. I had to put it ahead of romance. The chance of discovering something about my father came before the chance I had with Jessica.

A few days later, I heard from others at the staff hostel that Jessica's ex-boyfriend had come to work at Aviemore, and I began to suspect she was cheating on me, and that when she'd asked me about cheating, she had been asking more about herself, not him. One night I climbed the stairs to her room, determined to know the truth.

'Why are you avoiding me?' I called out. I was standing by her door and she wouldn't let me in.

'Please, Kári, let's talk about this later. I'm tired,' she whispered back through the doorframe.

'Just let me in for a second.'

'No. Go to bed. I promise, we'll talk about this in the morning.' But I heard a second voice from inside.

'Who's that with you?' I asked.

'No-one. It's nothing. Go to bed. Please, go.'

I was drunk, but I trusted my hunch that she was with someone. It was infidelity, and my first encounter with that grasping ache of jealousy. The next morning I asked her what was happening.

'Who was that in your room?' I said.

'It was nothing,' she said. 'Brian's got a job here, that's all. He and I were talking last night. It wasn't a good time to see you. I didn't want to see the two of you fighting.'

'Are you leaving me?'

'Kári, you're leaving me.'

'I'm just going to Iceland for a month. I can come back.'

'You'll have forgotten me in a week. There must be lots of pretty girls in Iceland.'

'What are you talking about? Why are you always accusing me of thinking about other women? You're the one who had Brian in your room last night.' She put her hand up to stop me saying more.

'Come to me when you come back, if you really mean it.'

The following night, Jessica and Brian came to the club. They were drunk. They danced, touched. He stroked the second-best perm in the world.

'What the fuck does he think he's doing here?' asked Jason.

'Don't worry about it,' I said.

'I will fucking worry about it.' He stepped across to Alex and the others. They fanned out. I felt sick. Jason came back.

'Just say the word. We'll kill him.'

10

LOVERS

It was with the offer of Brian's destruction still lingering with me that I travelled to Iceland. It wasn't my style to have Brian killed—neither the violence nor the urgency—I would rather have Jessica back. I left Scotland afraid that Jason would take matters into his own hands, but he never did. He later told me that it was the first time he stopped himself.

As soon as I arrived in Reykjavík, the army of secretaries swung into action and urged me to find my father immediately. Nanci had maintained her anger at the unknown man during our years away, and she said that I should 'at least get some money out of the bastard'. Each morning, after she'd cooked me breakfast and lit me one of her thin, dark More's, she reminded me where the phone was. Eventually, I picked it up and, the week after I had toured the highlands in a minibus of patriots and amateur linguists, Gísli and I had our drive to the president's lodge. It was when I agreed to keep the secret for him.

Why did I agree to keep his secret and in turn accept that

it was also mine? Why did I allow them to remain secret lovers, and not insist that they be parents together? At the time, my answer to myself was that I was afraid to upset them. Ultimately, that may be the only real answer there is. My fears were well founded and broad based: there was Gísli's wife, and their children, and my mother's promise, and what I supposed was their enduring love. I also didn't want to endanger any chance I had with him in the future, and to this end I was prepared to do almost anything he asked. Keeping him secret seemed a small price to pay for having him. He said he would remember my birthday, and at the time that seemed a gain.

If there is more to it than that—more to it than the fears and needs of a child—then I think it is that I was burdened by an old-fashioned idea, one that I am only now beginning to understand. It was my sense of honour towards Gísli, and my inescapable belief in the love of one's father. It must sound ludicrous, I know, for me to be honouring the absent father in this way. I suppose, that's what it means to be seventeen—one is always a little ludicrous at that age. Or that's what it means to be seventeen in Iceland, where things are always at once simpler and more complete. The point is that I wanted to do the right thing, by both my parents and my country. I wanted to do the loving thing and, in 1990, it seemed positively wrong to be the ruin of his family life. I couldn't take responsibility for that in quite the same way I could take responsibility for my life, and his absence in it.

I left him that day telling myself that I'd found out everything I needed to know. It wouldn't be possible for me to move back to Iceland—the law stood in the way of that. Gísli didn't want me there, either, and I was sure he wouldn't help me get around the law. But Gísli was in love with my mother and, at the time, that seemed crucial, even the main thing to me. It meant that my mother had probably been in love with him, and I doubted that she was capable of falling out of love.

Gísli was the flirty kind, certainly, but I believed him when he said that he'd only ever loved Mum and his wife, because in so many ways it helped make sense of the promise, or at least its longevity. He hadn't wanted to lose either of them, and openness would have forced him to make a choice. Who, I thought, was to say that you couldn't be in love with two women at once? Wasn't that a social rule rather than a rule of the heart?

There was nothing to connect my parents now but me, and I flew out of Reykjavík in low spirits, convinced that I had failed but unsure of how. I didn't want to leave, and I worried that all I'd done by visiting was prolong and intensify my sense of loss.

In London, I found a message from Jessica telling me she'd left Brian again, and moved to Buckinghamshire. She was doing hairdressing; I should visit her, if I wanted. She spotted my arrival from the salon window, and ran out and jumped on me, covering me with kisses.

'Thank God you're here,' she said. 'I'm so sorry for what I did in Aviemore. I was an arsehole. Brian's an arsehole. He did the dirty on me again. I'm sorry.' She didn't ask me whether I'd met anyone in Iceland, and I thought this very self-possessed of her. Maybe she sensed I hadn't come close to any women under fifty—the army of secretaries had virtually been my only female company.

We walked to a nearby hotel and checked in as a married couple—why such an elaborate cover I'm not sure. It was 1990, for goodness sake. Then, she insisted on dinner. I must have frowned a little because she asked, 'What's the rush?' She was the rush, I responded.

'Eat first, Kári,' she said. 'You're so thin.'

'I don't know why,' I said. 'Nanci's been feeding me eggs every morning for a month.'

'Did you see him?'

'Yes, I saw him. It was no good. He's a coward. He was terrified of me.'

'He's just a man,' said Jessica, between mouthfuls of English–Italian pub fare.

'Me, too, remember. And I'm doing just what he wants. Keeping quiet. And at the same time, I've been awful to you.'

'But I knew you wouldn't stay. You told me you would go back.'

'But what if I'm in love? Shouldn't I stay?'

She didn't reply.

'Did you hear me?' I asked quietly. 'I think I'm in love.'

'There you go,' she said after a moment. 'You said it.'

We finished our dinner in silence. Then she laid it out for me.

'This is corny, but I have to tell you what a friend said to me once. She said, "Love is like a bus. You wait and wait, and then you see a big truck, and you think it's the bus. And then you see the bus, and you know it's the bus." It's not poetry, Kári, but it's true. If you think you're in love, you're not in love. You should keep travelling.'

'But what about you?' It was a vague question. The one I wanted to ask was, why didn't she say that she was in love, too? Even if was just a thought.

'Look me up when you get back,' she replied at last. 'Tell me if you know any better then.'

It didn't occur to me to ask her along. I was too preoccupied with the idea of being in love to really do anything about it. Better to reflect, to write poetry, and to leave. Better to be endlessly concerned with notions of love than to ask a beautiful girl to leave a shitty job and catch the ferry with me to Belgium.

Mum was right, after all. I was just like my father, and never sure how to act. Instead, I worried and made love to Jessica, felt sorry for myself, and two days later caught the train to Dover. So, that was the kind of lover I was.

11

FALLING OFF HORSES

Journeys home are several. My meeting with my father was one, while the month I spent in Iceland, with the trip into the interior and up to the north, another. And now I returned to Brisbane for a third journey home, and in many respects the most effectual, because it was during the next nine years, when I didn't leave Australia at all, that I began to complicate my childhood in Iceland with a different, and more adult, kind of curiosity, and one that opened up a whole new way of belonging.

For, in my very first class at university, I found myself taken home. My tutor, Martin, looked up from his roll and asked whether Kári wasn't an Icelandic name.

'Yes, it is,' I answered.

'As in Kári in *Njál's Saga*?' he continued, a little shocked.

'Yes, I think that's where it comes from,' I said. 'I haven't read the saga myself.'

'Fancy that,' said Martin. 'I've been to Iceland twice.'

He had been drawn there by the sagas, the medieval

Icelandic accounts of life during the Viking age—the very texts that Ed had brought with him to Iceland in 1972. He knew a lot more about them than I did. I was embarrassed to admit to him that I hadn't read a saga yet. That wasn't a problem, he said, I could study them in Brisbane. The next year I enrolled with about twenty others in Martin's Old Icelandic course. I couldn't believe my luck.

Martin's favourite was *The Saga of Gísli*, the story of a warrior–poet outlawed for killing his brother-in-law. Martin often spoke of wanting to 'meet' Gísli, my father's tenth-century namesake, in the setting of the saga.

'I didn't get to Dyrafjörður when I was in Iceland,' he went on. This was Gísli the Outlaw's home deep in the Westfjords, the remotest part of the country, a place Mum had visited during her voyage around the island on *The Esja*.

'I ran out of time on my car rental,' continued Martin, 'and had to return to Reykjavík. I'll get there one day, though.' When I told him that I'd never made it to the Westfjords either, he joked, 'You'll have to be my guide the next time I go.'

In the meantime, Martin was very much my guide, and the Iceland of the sagas, for hundreds of years the focus of scholarly enquiry, took its place alongside the Iceland of my childhood. In a way it was another surrogate for the Iceland that lived on while I was in Brisbane. It was a heady mix because the sagas were, like me, nostalgic for better, simpler times, when people knew the right thing to do, and how to act.

It was Martin's way of reading them that helped us to become friends. He treated the sagas as a perfect universe, islands apart in which you found yourself moving beyond yourself. I recognised myself in his relationship with the sagas. The interior otherworld he showed us was what I had created at Mostyn House, when I began to treat stories as rooms that lay beyond the control of the school. I think it was also what Mum had found in travelling. It was a way of encountering the world and accepting its complexity.

Just as Martin wanted to meet the Gísli of the sagas, I found myself reading very closely for characters that I thought I recognised. In Laxdæla saga, I encountered Guðrún Ósvifursdóttir, a young woman from the mid-west of Iceland who falls in love with Kjartan. He wants to go abroad, as do all young Icelandic heroes, to prove himself at the court of the Norwegian king. He leaves with his best friend Bolli, with a request to Guðrún for her to wait for him for three years. When only Bolli returns, she thinks the worst—Kjartan has fallen in love with someone else—and she marries Bolli instead. But Kjartan does return. He was just running late, and now he has to look elsewhere for a wife. He has brought with him magnificent presents, which he gives to his new bride. Consumed by jealousy, Guðrún manufactures a feud, and then demands that Bolli kill his old friend. On one of the hill-clipped valleys of the Dales district, Bolli ambushes his Kjartan and murders him.

Many years later, when Guðrún is old, she turns to religion. She establishes the first convent in Iceland, at Helgafell or Holy Mountain, on Snæfellnes. This is the same peninsula Mum's boat rounded as the fog cleared, when Jón had come down to her cabin to borrow the camera. Guðrún's son Bolli, the son of the killer Bolli, comes to see her there.

'Tell me one thing, Mother,' he asks, 'whom did you love most?'

She doesn't really want to answer him. But he presses her for a response. Then, she says, 'I was worst to the one I loved the most.' And that is all she'll tell him: like my mother did a long time later, Guðrún insisted on silence, or the veiled silence of an evasive response. 'He was clean and I was lonely.' And, rather like Bolli before me, I had to make what meaning I could from that hint alone.

Our next work was *Egil's Saga*, and sure enough, there was Gísli, my father. Egil can't get along with his father. At a young age he is packed off abroad, seemingly a default, medieval solution for the difficult and heroic young men that Viking society produced. He travels to the courts of northern Europe and, through his skill as a poet, crafts a place for himself in the retinues of kings and chieftains.

Poets were prized in medieval Scandinavia. They were the propagandists of the day, recording the deeds and qualities of their leaders. And the most difficult poetic form to master was the skaldic poem, an intricate style that demanded great skill in the use of metaphor and grammatical construction.

Iceland is an island of poets, but of fishermen too. And this, of course, means that young men die. When Egil's son is drowned, he locks himself away in a private room and refuses to eat or drink. He can't go on. He prefers to share in his son's fate. And his daughter Thordís asks to join him. She too would like to die. Egil is pleased that someone else understands him, and lets her in.

'Well done, my daughter,' he says. 'We will die together.'

'Yes. But one thing,' she responds, 'you must compose a poem for your son before you die. It would be wrong to leave him without one. Drink this cup of milk so you have the strength for it.'

It is a trick, of course, but a productive one. Egil empties the cup, and then composes '*Sonatorrek*', or his 'Lament for the Son'. It's his most famous poem, and it begins with these two verses.

My mouth strains
To move the tongue,
To weigh and wing
The choice word:
Not easy to breathe
Odin's inspiration
In my heart's hinterland,
Little hope there.

My sorrow the source
Of the sluggard stream
Mind-meandering,
This heavy word-mead,
Poet's power
Gold-praised, that
Odin from ogres tore
In ancient time.

When Egil feels his poetic craft coming back, there is a recovery, and soon the poem's focus turns from the lost son to the father. The poem becomes a celebration of the poet's own life, and indeed the role of poetry—gradually creation takes the place of loss. And so, when Egil finishes the poem, he feels he must perform it to the household. Otherwise, it will be lost. The suicide pact has been undone, and Egil is once again able to see himself as a member of the family.

And I, of course, was Gunnar of Hlíðarendi, only the most famous and daring of all the saga characters. He appears in *Njál's Saga* alongside my namesake, Kári Sölmundarson. There are obvious reasons why Gunnar is popular, and why he has long captured the imagination of saga readers. He is fair, handsome, and agile. A great fighter and a bowman, and clearly a favourite among women. He swims like a seal. Almost a comic touch: he can jump as far backward as he can forward. He doesn't mount his horse like other Vikings. Instead he runs up to it and uses his halberd to launch him into position.

Too good, almost. If ever a character needed a flaw to be sympathetic rather than just irritating, it is Gunnar of Hlíðarendi, and so the author of *Njál's Saga* gives him three.

First, he falls in love with Hallgerð Longlegs, the most beautiful woman of her generation, but also the most fatal. Her first two husbands have been killed because of her, and Gunnar will, in part, die as a result of her obstinacy. She steals cheese from a neighbouring farm. Gunnar strikes her for it, and she vows to remember the blow.

Second, Gunnar dislikes killing more than other men do. This is a problem for a Viking, and particularly for one as able in the art of killing as Gunnar. He will always be challenged by his contemporaries, simply because he is so good.

Third, Gunnar ignores the warning of his most prescient friend, Njál, who tells him, firstly, that he must never kill twice in the same family, and, secondly, that if he does, he must accept whatever settlement is made for him by men of good will.

Of course, Gunnar does kill twice in the same family. The settlement made for him is to leave Iceland for three years, a sentence known at the time as lesser outlawry. As he and his brother, Kolskeg, ride towards the sea, where a ship waits to take them abroad, Gunnar's horse trips and throws him. He looks up from the ground, back to his farm Hlíðarendi, and says: 'How lovely the slopes are, more lovely than they have ever seemed to me before, golden cornfields and new-mown hay. I am going back home, and I will not go away.'

Shortly after, his enemies attack. For a long while, he is able to keep them at bay with his bow. Then his bowstring snaps. 'Hallgerð,' he calls out, 'let me have some of your hair. I need it for my bow.'

'Does much depend on it?' she asks.

'My life depends on it.'

'In that case, let me remind you of the time you struck me. I refuse.'

And that was the end of Gunnar.

Waiting produces its own energy, I'm sure, and I found I was forever telling myself to be ready. For what, I wasn't sure. I changed my enrolment from straight Arts to Arts/Law, and exchanged the sagas for lists of cases and statutes. The law was concerned with language, yes, but never for its own sake, and I ended up mixing with other law students who didn't really suit the subject—frustrated musicians, writers, sportsmen even. They all came out of the exclusive schools, mainly Brisbane Boys Grammar, and had a preoccupation with The Smiths, The Housemartins, and Martin Amis—just about anything English, in fact. All flicked hair and end-of-the-world sarcasm.

Clayton was my entry point into this world of middle-class angst. He responded to the anger that I felt growing within me about Gísli, because, like me, he enjoyed being angry and didn't really know what to do about it. Clayton sang like Morrissey, flicked his hair, and had formed a band made up of him and some med students. They watched *Ren and Stimpy* religiously and ironically, and smoked a packet of Marlboro Reds every day, like me. The credo was 'be musicians, and do a law degree in your spare time'. We were, we thought, fucked-up but friendly. Or, not too unfriendly.

For me, it was a period of increasing introspection, and I have often thought of my twenties as alternating between learning about others' achievements and despair at my own. Certainly, I changed from the gregarious boy whom Mum had likened to Gísli into someone more earnest and certainly less pleasant to be with. I now interpreted my part in the promise to Gísli's secret as simple cowardice. I once mentioned to Clayton about Icelandic patronymics, and how I thought I might one day take Gíslason as my middle name—literally 'son of Gísli'—if it were ever practical to do so; perhaps after Gísli died.

'Your initials would be K.G.,' he noticed. 'How perfect for you: Cagey Reid.'

I had forgotten how to be charming, and I suppose like a lot of men in their early twenties, I had become awkward and fairly unappealing. But then, the law girls were mainly unappealing, too. You could already see them in silver four-wheel drives. There was a splinter group, a small, politically minded collaborative who formed WATL, Women and the Law. I had been at the first international women's strike with Mum back in 1975, so it seemed okay to attend.

'What are you doing here?' asked one of them, Alyssa, when I strolled in.

'This is WATL, isn't it?' She said it was. 'Well, I'm here for that.'

'Why? I wouldn't have thought someone like you would want to hang out with a bunch of feminists.'

'What if I'm a feminist, too?' I asked.

'That seems unlikely. Do you and Clayton spend your evenings talking about police interrogation of assault victims? Or is female circumcision more the topic of choice? Tell me. I'm fascinated.'

'Is that the test for being a feminist?'

'You guys don't seem too worried, that's all. It's going your way, isn't it? It must be good to have a dick.'

'The law hasn't done me that many favours,' I responded. 'Nor my mother, I don't think.'

'Why don't you tell me about that, then. Where are you coming from, Kári?'

I liked her. The accusatory tone was good. I needed it. She

was the first girl since Jessica who told me that I was wrong. Every day, in fact. And it didn't much matter about what. I was wrong about sex, family life, food, even cigarettes. It was better to roll your own, she said. And, yes, it was.

We began a relationship that would take me through the whole of my law degree, and my honours and masters years, when I finally realised that I was never going to make a good lawyer and returned to literature. And yet, we never quite managed to give our relationship a name. It was my fault. I set it up to be one of those relationships that would spend its life working out what it was, and most often what it couldn't be. I couldn't commit, but I couldn't just be friends. That type of thing.

'What is it that you want then?' she would say, repeatedly.

'I'm not sure. What sort of a question is that, anyway?' I answered. 'I want to do a PhD and I want to be an academic. I want to be a musician. I want to relearn Icelandic. I want to be with you, you know that.'

'Every girl you ever know will be a hostage to Iceland. Why don't you just go and live there? There's nothing keeping you in Brisbane. There's no rule that says you have to stay. You, of all people, should know that.'

'Like I said, I want to start a PhD.'

'And you have your mum, right? In Brisbane.'

'I'm not doing a PhD for my mum.'

'Are you sure? Just about everything you do is for her.'

'Why do you have to bring this up?'

'Well, that's why you're such a fuck-up. That's why. Why don't you just call your father and tell him that you're going to end the secret? Don't wait to go there. Stop waiting. Do you think someone's going to come and pick you up and say: here's your father, he loves you after all?'

It seemed hard, but I had sometimes said harder things to her. It was the way we were together, dark and direct. Often fucked-up and often unfriendly.

'You're scared of her, scared of this secret that she passed down to you,' she went on. 'And that's why you're scared of me. That's why you're scared of women.'

'Don't be ridiculous,' I said. 'You scare me in a million other ways.'

'Good,' she said.

It was all coming to a head, it seemed, but where would it end? Once, when I visited Mum and found she wasn't home, I stood waiting on the thin cement walkway that ran along the doors of the apartment block. I was taking in the view over the western suburbs of Brisbane, towards the D'Aguilar Range, always hazy in the afternoons. And then I was looking down to the ground some way beneath me.

'Am I a suicide?' I asked myself, as though I existed apart from my own consciousness, as though a second self was lying against the ground far beneath me.

But it wasn't my death that I needed, it was merely my father's, in a manner of speaking. The spiral that was reaching its base ended with him. He was gone, just as he had never really been. It was the promise of fidelity and honour that had made him a father, and now I sensed that a different outlook was forming within me. It was a way of seeing Iceland that related the country to Australia, my mother, and me, rather than to his absence in our lives. The bridge to Iceland wasn't Gísli, after all—I understood that now. If I returned to Iceland again, it could not be to find him.

The chance finally came in 1999, nine years after I had met my father at the president's lodge. I began a doctorate in medieval Icelandic literature. As part of my early research, my university agreed to send me to Iceland for two months. The minute I received the news that I could go, I decided on two things, or at least decided that two things lay before me. I needed to go to Hlíðarendi, where Gunnar had made his decision to stay in Iceland, and I needed to meet my siblings, Gísli's other children.

Unexpectedly, news then arrived that Gísli was unwell. He had Parkinson's disease. My mother worried that it was genetic, and that I might be at risk, while I worried that it might be the end of any chance I had of disrupting the promise. Had I left it too long to break my word? More news came, that was out of date and out of order with his life in Iceland. His business had collapsed and there was a row, some kind of legal dispute, between the partners of his firm. Apparently, Gísli had lost his house because of money problems. And Ólafur, one of Gísli's sons with his wife Ólöf, had died. A criminal case against the boy's friends had ensued. The news was muddled: it came indirectly and unclearly. But it looked as though my father's world was falling apart.

Around the same time letters arrived about Gunnar and Lilja, too. The first envelope contained letters from both Lilja and her granddaughter Björk, the one who'd enchanted me with her perm.

December 16. '98

My dearest Susan,

Thank you for all your letters during the years. It has been a long time since I've responded to them, but now my granddaughter Björk is writing for me.

Now there is darkness in my life. You knew Gunnar had heart disease and was waiting for an operation. Well, in the morning of November 23, I went to the hospital because my health was not good and Gunnar had had a call from his hospital two weeks earlier that he should come the following day. So it was fine because then he didn't have to worry about me alone at home these three days that I should be away. But it goes to my heart to tell you that he died a few hours after the operation, on the 24th.

I feel like an empty person, it was so unexpected. My health is very poor but fortunately I could go to the funeral. It was difficult but I had to, so I did. I don't know anything about how my health is going to be, how long I will be here and where I'm going to be in the future. Our little house will be standing empty for some time, I'm afraid.

I hope you will keep in touch, you can send me letters addressed to Björk.

I send my best regards to Kári and ask the Lord to keep you both and thank you for everything.

Lilja

Dear Susan,

I want to write you a little note from myself. My grandma is taking all this by some incredible inner strength. Of course

she cries a lot when she is alone but she doesn't want us to
see that. She is very sick now and we don't know if she can
be with us for a few hours on Christmas Eve, but we hope
so. We're all going to be at Lilja's home.

There is a lack of Christmas spirit in the family, it has
been a difficult year for us. But life goes on and we know
that both my dearest grandfathers will look after us.

I want to thank you for your loyalty to my
grandparents and hope you will send grandma news from
you in the future.

I hope you and Kári will have a wonderful Christmas
time and wish you a happy new year.
Björk

A second letter came not long after the first, it was from Björk.

14.03.99

Dear Susan and Kári,
I am sorry that I have not written earlier, but I have to tell
you the tragic news that grandmother Lilja died on January
28th.

After grandfather's death her condition worsened and
she was never able to return home. During the last weeks
it became clear that a recovery was unlikely but her spirits
remained high.

She remained alert and had full consciousness until
the last few hours. My mother stayed at her side until
grandmother found her peace. She was never in pain and
was up and about until the last week.

Unfortunately she had passed away when Kári's letter arrived, but she often mentioned both of you and how much she valued your friendship and loyalty to her and grandfather.

If Kári puts the song he wrote in grandfather's memory on a disc, I would like very much to buy the disc.

Finally I would like to express my gratitude to both of you for the dear friendship you showed my grandparents for all the years. I know it meant a lot to them.

I wish you both all the best for the future.

Yours sincerely,

Björk

Of all my mother's friends, Gunnar and Lilja had been the least concerned about why she'd ended up in Iceland, or why she'd protected Gísli. Perhaps that is why they are still my heroes, and why as a parent I now understand that their generosity towards us was a parent's generosity: it was unambiguous, non-mysterious, and calm. They had never shown any concern about my background, and in this omission they silently expressed what I still think are the twin rules of Icelandic society, the rules that my mother's boss Garðar had once tried to teach her: all children are welcome, and we all have the right to stand alone. This, I have come to realise, is the paradox at the heart of so many things Icelandic: you are totally owned and totally on your own.

There were exceptions, of course. My father didn't quite think all children were welcome, and the law had long fallen out of touch with common sentiment. But perhaps my brother and sisters would, and perhaps they would have enough of an independent spirit to make up their own minds about me. It was possible that they hadn't inherited their father's hesitancy, and instead still believed, as Gunnar and Lilja had, that the circumstances were never as important as the results.

Strange as it might sound, I firmly believed that at Hlíðarendi I would find an answer to what ailed me. I was convinced that this place, a remnant of the saga era, was the link between a life of waiting in Brisbane and a homecoming in Iceland. I had to find that spot where Gunnar had fallen off his horse, and had looked up the slope, and had decided to stay. Because that's how you did it, I thought. That's how you made decisions. Where did you find a horse like that, one that would throw you at just the right moment, except at Hlíðarendi?

The night before I left for Reykjavík, my mother and I had dinner at a café near the university. She was fifty-eight now; nearly thirty years had passed since she had first arrived in Iceland. She had returned to Iceland only once since we'd moved to Brisbane, and although she disliked the changes that had occurred while we'd been away, it remained holy ground for her; that much was clear. She handed me a list of addresses comprising the contact details of the army of secretaries and an annotated outline of all the places we'd lived—information she had kept at hand for the moment I began to make my own way back. It started with the basement apartment at Sólvallagata, where she'd arrived on that windy afternoon in December 1970.

Naturally, she was the one who best understood what drew me back. But even between us, the feeling for Iceland seemed an almost inexpressible inner empathy, which because it was inexpressible, most often came to be communicated and commemorated in everyday lists like these. We agreed there was no escape. We agreed we would probably always be going back. What I didn't mention to her that night was that I'd more or less decided to break the promise to Gísli.

12

TO HLÍÐARENDI

Openness, when it came, took me by surprise, and unsteadied me like vertigo. I was in London for a stopover. I had put my bags in at the left luggage in Liverpool Street Station and had made an uneven line across town to Bloomsbury. I was visiting the Department of Scandinavian Studies at University College. The entrance was at the back. I creaked along the floorboards to a reception area, wondering whether there were any scholars in residence.

'No, I'm afraid the teaching staff are seldom here in summer,' the receptionist told me. She waited for me to leave. But, as I was eyeing off some books that were stacked for sale on the front counter, she added, 'Our Icelandic doctoral student, Svanhildur, is here, though. It's just that she's very busy. She's making the finishing touches to her thesis.'

'Do you think she would mind if I popped my head in?'

'I'll check, but don't keep her long.'

The warm day, and a view of the bright trees on the other side of Gower Street, came in through a window behind

Svanhildur's desk. She was dressed for a hot London day, but all her manners were Icelandic: she stood up, shook hands, and asked me to sit down as though it were about time I'd come to visit.

I was at the start of my doctoral research and Svanhildur at the very end of hers, making the final changes to her dissertation. To me, she had all the ease and fluency of a big name. She replied to my queries about the sagas by asking her own about my years in Iceland, and my family there. Her firm curiosity brought me yet another step closer to Reykjavík. It was the villager's interest that is inscribed into all conversations in Iceland.

'When did you leave Iceland?' she asked.

'When I was ten.'

'Your mother's Icelandic?'

'No, she's English, actually.'

'I thought that, as your surname is an English one, you must have an English father.'

'It's a bit complicated.'

'That's not unusual in Iceland,' she replied. 'But what's your father's name, then?'

'Gísli Ólafsson,' I heard myself say, even before I could think to stop.

She didn't know him. I steered the conversation back to the sagas and left the building laden with a bag of books that I would have to leave, during my travels to Iceland, with Shane and Fiona, friends from Brisbane who lived in Norwich and were putting me up for a couple of nights. I had known them for years, but not even they knew who my father was. And here

I was telling a complete stranger, and an Icelander at that, who in passing conversation could quite easily begin a chain of information that would end not only with my father but half of Iceland as well. How easy it all was. Maybe there was no need to be tossed from a horse, after all.

This sudden openness about my father was accompanied by an overwhelming feeling of coming home before I was really ready for it. It enveloped me on the plane, when the Icelandic voices of the other passengers met me like the first sound of waves at the beginning of a holiday. Their voices washed across the aisles, searching out friends and relatives.

'*Nei, blessaður!*' I would hear, and that would begin a fresh round of disbelief that someone from Iceland had bumped into someone else from Iceland, here, on a plane in London, of all places.

In the seat next to me sat James, who was bringing his mother home. She was, he said, in the cargo hold below.

'Actually, the whole family's on the plane. My girlfriend's just over there.' He pointed behind us towards the nervous smile of a girl who sat five rows back. 'The rest are up at the back.' After a pause, he added, 'Mum put aside for all of us to come.'

I told James a little of my own story, how I was also doing something for my parents on this trip. He replied that we were lucky to have the need of a return.

Our flight split Britain length-wise, and so James and I took turns in identifying the cities of the Midlands, the Lakes District, and inlets of the west coast of Scotland as we passed over. One of those little dots down there, I thought, must be

Ullapool, where Jessica had driven me, and where I had told her I would leave her for Iceland. A couple of hours later I could see the black lava rock and red mountains of Iceland.

We descended over the cracked landscape of the south, following the headland of steam and craters until we were level with them. I wished James the best for the funeral as I saw Patricia standing in the front row of onlookers on the other side of a glass divide. She hadn't changed at all; still a fat Sydney girl in unquantifiable middle age, with a big, chiny smile, artist's eyes, and a large stance. She filled the drive to Reykjavík with the same exuberant telling of events—stories of her dogs and cats, and reviews of local art shows—as she had when I was a boy.

I was more distracted by the lava field around us than I had ever been. It extended for miles to our right, while on our left, on the narrow strip of land between the road and the ocean, rocky outcrops of lava formed jagged walls around clear ponds, grass ovals, and the occasional house and abandoned farm. Keilir, one of the volcanoes responsible for all this, stood over its work on the far right of us. The sky was bright and we soon caught our first glimpse of Reykjavík, the cathedral Hallgrímskirkja. After decades of construction it was finished at last, and around it surfaced the thin line of blue-grey concrete houses and the luxurious waterside homes of the outskirts. Already, I knew that I was returning for good, and that even if this was a visit, it was the beginning of reclamation. It was so obvious: the missing piece in me was simply the feeling of being in Iceland.

On this trip I was staying with Bergur, the old friend of my mother's who had once drunkenly declared himself to be my father, and his wife Rut. She and her eldest daughter, Kolbrún, met me at the door of their mansion by the sea. Nervous, attractive, formal, they welcomed me with handshakes, hesitant smiles, and implorations about taking off my jacket, which by now looked like something I'd picked up off the road. And where was the rest of my luggage?

'This is all I've brought,' I replied. 'I know it doesn't look like it holds much. But carpetbags are like that, aren't they?'

'Oh dear,' said Rut, looking sympathetically towards the bag. 'How is Susan?' she then asked. 'I can see her in your eyes.'

'Really? Funny. Mum's always said I look like my father.'

'Oh. But there's a lot of your mother there.'

Patricia and I were taking off our shoes at the front door as Bergur stepped down from upstairs. His round, boyish face wore a pensive look.

'Am I late for something?' he asked.

'Bergur, you knew Kári was coming today,' said Rut.

'Did I? Very well. Welcome home, Kári *minn*,' he said. 'Rut tells me you're going to be staying with us for a couple of months. Whatever Rut thinks. Best to go along with that.'

'Thank you.'

'You've become a saga scholar then?' he asked, as he led me upstairs into the house.

'Oh, barely. I've started a doctorate.'

'You know our Njála, of course.' 'Njála' was the affectionate nickname given to *Njál's Saga*.

'*Njál's Saga* is probably why I'm here,' I replied.

'Yes?' Bergur again looked apprehensive. 'I know that part of Iceland,' he continued, 'around the southern farmlands near Oddi. I worked there as a boy. I still go fishing there every summer. I can afford it now. You know, when I was younger, the farmers just let us fish for nothing. But that was before we realised we liked salmon.'

'I want to travel there,' I answered, 'especially around Hlíðarendi.'

'Gunnar's farm. I expect I could take you there. I know the way.'

'Please, I would adore that.'

There was coffee, pancakes, Icelandic doughnuts, and three or four types of cake. The full Icelandic welcome: total coffee time. Their house was very large. On the ocean side, it was split-levelled, with a living room enclosed by glass windows and, downstairs, an apartment on its own, with a line of bedrooms that faced out to the fjord. Mine would be Kolbrún's old room, which she had now left for an apartment of her own. It was furnished with a single bed, a writing desk, and a stereo; everything you needed.

The tide was coming in. Walkers, bike riders, and roller-bladers passed by at different speeds. Patricia was much taken with a large, bronze bird that stood twenty metres from the ocean wall, one of a number of sculptures along the path.

'Oh, that bird,' she kept saying. 'What a wonderful work.'

'They are extinct now,' said Bergur, addressing me. 'We killed those ones off.' Then, 'The path runs all the way to Seltjarnarnes,' pointing his fingers behind him. 'I try never to use it.'

It was a joke, presented with the same bleak countenance as he had used to welcome me. The bike path was a very lovely one, and I guessed from Rut's sigh that they went out on it often.

'Is it a long way to walk?' I asked. I knew Seltjarnarnes was where Gísli had lost his house and so, of course, I was curious.

'A little way,' Rut replied. 'You can use the car when it's free,' she then offered.

For the next hour, we spoke about my stay and how I'd fill in my time. Soon, their other children, my namesake, Kári, who was a few years older than me, and their youngest daughter, Rakel, would be back from holidays abroad. Kári, they said, would want to take me into the country—he was the outdoors type. And there were other visitors expected, too, a family of five Icelandic descendants from Vancouver. The grandmother of that group was called Mildred, just like my grandmother, and she was returning to Iceland for the first time in decades.

I asked how far it was to the local swimming pool. I'd been so looking forward to swimming again in Iceland.

'Vesturbæjarlaug is walking distance from here,' said Rut, 'about twenty minutes.'

'Would it be rude if I go now?' I asked.

'Not at all,' she replied, but perhaps a little too hesitantly, I thought. But I took the opening and thanked them for the welcome and rushed out, over a grass mound that was used as a fence for the back of their yard, and onto the path.

It was already eight o'clock, but still busy on the path. Roller-blading children were collapsing onto the ground like folding chairs. Light aircraft was approaching from the northwest, chugging breathlessly towards the landing strips of the domestic airport. On the balcony of one of the white houses along Ægisíða, a seafront street running beside the path, a family watched over all the outdoor activity. The ocean played lightly against the black rocks, and an old fishing shed standing next to a small, dry-docked fishing tug and drying lines was silhouetted by the reflected sun. Near to it was another of the public sculptures, a stone haddock that looked as though it was thrown out of a bucket onto the ground.

I was joined on my walk by the uplifting feeling of good solitude that I remembered from when I was a child and had rowed into the quiet cove out of sight of Molly and Steini's summerhouse, or when I'd walked along the frozen track between our place and Molly's—a contented aloneness that I hadn't known since I was last here. It intensified my awareness of the volcanic landscape to the south, and the outline of peninsulas to the north. How could I leave this?

At the pool, the receptionist flicked a blue, rubber key band on the counter and the automatic swinging door opened.

'*Daginn*,' I said.

'*Góðan daginn*,' she replied, looking over her glasses as though she were expecting me to get on with a point. I had forgotten just how severe that look could be, the Icelandic frown. Her gaze narrowed. It said that she had stopped expecting a point.

I left her for the showers downstairs. On the change-room wall was a line drawing of a human figure with five areas of special concern that had been shaded in: the two armpits, the groin, and the two feet. These, said the poster, were to be washed with care. I obeyed and washed my shaded-in areas before dashing across the cold cement outside to the pool.

The tourist brochures call Iceland a country of fire and ice. It is a cliché, but here it seemed true, as I suppose it was in the highland interior, where the volcanoes and glaciers meet. Like the country around them, the people at first seem severe, but occasionally they reveal the typically molten, inner life of the Scandinavians. The pools bring it out of you, and the old people in particular move quite quickly from exchanging greetings to discussing their personal lives. It is a process that seems unbroken from the drunken confessions of farm dances and summer celebrations. Perhaps it is the hot water: it releases emotions into the cold air. Or the proximity created by the shape of the hot pots, which are small, round and most often crowded. They line the main lap pools, which is slightly cooler, and form the first port of call once you've done your exercise. You are only really home again in Iceland after you've had your first swim.

When I got back, Bergur said we should take a drive downtown to look at all the changes since I'd last visited.

'You know Laugarnes?' he asked. 'From Njála.' He looked at me, but I couldn't remember. 'Hallgerð died there. There is a plaque in her memory.' She had moved to the area after Gunnar's death, her refuge during the ignominy that followed from not helping her husband in his final moments. I said something about it being unusual to commemorate such a famous villain in this way.

'No, she is just a good Icelandic woman,' replied Bergur. 'It's wrong to read her as a villain. They do very well without us. And they are proud. Gunnar should have known that.'

'But she let him be killed.'

'Yes, of course she did. But she also loved him.'

We joined a procession of cars. In front of us, someone stopped to chat to a friend they'd spotted on the pavement. The traffic slowed to walking pace, a Saturday night driving circle. A beautiful girl dressed in a short skirt walked past a small group of tourists heavily clad in jeans, boots and bright raincoats.

'They think Reykjavík is a whaling station,' said Bergur, speaking of the tourists. He kept asking me what I thought of all the changes. In fact, nothing had changed. The smells, the sounds, the feeling in the air, entire streets of association that made the drive seem like not only a return to Reykjavík but to a different time—I felt like I was aged nine again, and back on my paper run.

The descent of the street steepened as we entered an area of café bars, and then wound through the pretty, narrow streets that skirted Austurstræti near to Grjótagata, where Mum had worked when she first arrived. Each street was still an uninterrupted row of contorted, coloured houses, the style of homes that had been imported from Norway in the nineteenth century. As we came out at the harbour, there in front of us stood the unflinching black ocean and Mount Esja, still as imperious and sunlit as ever.

'*Esja okkar*,' said Bergur warmly, 'our Esja.'

Auden said on one of his visits that the sun might have settled on Iceland, but it was still visible on the mountains. So it was tonight at Laugarnes, with Esja seemingly illuminated from a hidden point. The sun also somehow discovered in the tips of the tall grass that now grew where Hallgerð had farmed, another woman stranded by the misfortune of having chosen the wrong man to love. Or, rather, of having not had a choice about love.

◄━►

María, a fresh-faced girl in black clogs, bounded out of the office and led me to the reading room.

'Will this do?' she asked, pointing to where I should sit.

'This is fantastic. Could I spend the afternoon here?' I was in Árnastofnun, the manuscript research institute, to begin my research.

'Have all month here, if you like. Just one thing,' she said, tapping her clogs against the door, 'the Norwegian president is visiting this afternoon. You'll have to stay in the reading room until he's gone.' I thought she was joking, and smiled. But she went on, 'Yes, I'm sorry. Perhaps if you want a coffee or need to go to the toilet you could do that in the next few minutes.'

Half an hour later, two heavily armed policemen with German shepherd dogs at their sides checked the reading room for bombs. After the policemen left, I settled down to a solitary afternoon amid the sagas, the slowly descending sun painting the book ends and the pale, wooden shelves. At five, María came in to say she was leaving for the day, and could I please let myself out. To me, this was heaven. I spent nearly every day of the next two months at the same desk.

I worked very hard on my thesis. For a break, I would spend the early evenings walking to the same swimming pool

I'd visited on my first night back, where I joined the regulars for a swim and a long stew in the hot pots. I was getting to know a few of them and, now and then, they'd pull me aside and demand an explanation of who I was and when I'd be coming back to Iceland to stay.

Then, I would retrace the path back to Bergur and Rut's for dinner and a beer in their open, bright living room. I walked along the sea path to their home, where my bedroom faced out to Skerjafjörður and Álftanes, where the president's lodge, Bessastaðir, stood out against the backdrop of the volcanic range. It was a symbol of lawfulness and national unity, and it was also a farm. Little wonder Gísli wanted to meet me there on my last visit; for him it stood for a rural aristocracy of which my family on his side had once formed a part. It was above all beautiful, and I loved to watch it glow in the afternoon light.

I also found myself wanting an alternative symbol. The office of president, after all, was such a recent invention, a role that had come only in the twentieth century. This was a country of stories much older than that.

In the living room, I would sit and meditate on a landscape painting that hung on Rut and Bergur's back wall. It was a study of Thingvellir, the national park near Reykjavík, by the Icelandic expressionist Johannes Kjarval. The perspective he'd adopted was along the ground, along the coloured rocks and the mosses, the berries and small flowers; a close and intimate point of view that told you that he loved the place he was painting, because he was so amongst it. The famous Thingvellir Lake and the bluffs around it are left aside for a moment, given over for the spaces between the rocks, where the minute life of damp, sheltered coves takes over.

I had met Thingvellir dozens of times in the sagas, but couldn't remember ever having gone there. It was the site of the first parliament, established in 930. It was also where the country adopted Christianity in 1000. And, in the thirteenth century, during the crisis years leading to Iceland's loss of independence, it was the place where it became obvious that the idea of an Icelandic nation was in disarray—the victim of a century of internal fights between the most powerful families. Thingvellir wouldn't fully re-emerge as a national ideal until the Romantic movement of the nineteenth century, when sovereignty began to be reclaimed.

It was an impressive and deeply symbolic history, but Thingvellir existed within a geology that spoke to you more profoundly than even human history could. In a series of deep rifts, Thingvellir revealed the meeting of the American and European continental plates, and the park surrounded a lake that had sunk during the area's seismic shifts. In a way, you could say that geology and history were at odds here—a breach in the earth's crust had become the symbol of national unity—yet, the result seemed inspiring rather than confusing.

I spent so much time sitting in front of Bergur and Rut's painting that, when I eventually got to visit the site with them, I found myself adopting Kjarval's point of view almost entirely. I wanted to walk among the crevices, the sheltered areas where travellers built their temporary booths and where people like Gunnar and Hallgerð might have met for the first time, and fallen in love. This was where she had asked him about his travels, and somewhere among the rifts he had asked her to sit down with him for their talk about court life in Norway.

Over the course of a very long day trip, we travelled to the area with the Canadian family who was also staying with Bergur and Rut. They were West Icelanders, a term given to the Canadian descendants of those who'd left Iceland in the nineteenth century. Our group filled two four-wheel drives, with Bergur taking me and the teenagers, whose optimistic parents told them to listen to us talk about the sagas, while in the other truck Rut travelled with the grandmother Mildred, her friend from a distant childhood year in Canada, Mildred's daughter, Carol, and son-in-law, Ralph.

Bergur, like me, wasn't going to launch into saga summaries if he thought that the two in the back were listening out of good-willed politeness. That seemed cruel. Instead, we offered them the front seat, and they took it in turns to sit with Bergur and guide us through their impressions. They noticed the small horses and the luxuries of life. Everyone, they said, dressed well, and everyone drove nice cars. It seemed such a rich country.

Bergur laughed. It was true, he said, Icelanders were rich. Now. But their comments took him back to the relative austerity of his youth, and of course its greater glamour. It seemed he had danced, fished, or been drunk at every farm in the southwest. His favourite horse used to walk him home. Once, during a storm, he got locked out of the fishing hut and his friends were too drunk to wake up to let him in.

'I nearly died that night,' he said with horror.

More pleasing, though, was that as the day went on these

recollections came to mingle with history, despite our good intentions of sparing the young from saga stories. Eventually I found myself being tested on the minor characters who'd lived at this or that farm. Bergur knew them all, because they were connected at some level to his own youthful misadventures, and to a sense of this countryside as the custodian of the past: his and Iceland's—the two weren't entirely separable. When he pointed out saga sites, the car lurched towards them, following the line of his distracted hands. We, too, nearly became part of the landscape.

At Thingvellir, Bergur and Rut, practiced in the art of the golden circle, a triangle of tourist traps near Reykjavík, left us at the top of the path and met us at the bottom. As we walked down, we looked for the outlines of the booths that had once populated the grass ledges. In among the thick clumps of summer grass, we found their nineteenth-century replicas. As with the Kjarval painting, history was best located at ground level.

We left Thingvellir for the road at the other side of the lake, bound for Laugarvatn, a small village with a school and surroundings of low woodlands and summerhouses—what the locals called a *sumarhúsasvæði* or 'summerhouse district'. We stopped for a swim in the school's training pool and then joined the busier road to Selfoss until we were at the turn-off for the wide valley of Thórsmörk. The glacier, Eyjafjallajökull, which all day had been an island of white light drawing us southwards, suddenly loomed above us, dirty and grey.

In a ruinous area of debris and broken ice, we met a line-up of cars waiting to ford a deep river. A small conference was in progress next to a bus fortified with enormous tyres and protection for the windows; the owners of the smaller vehicles were asking the bus driver for advice. Bergur went ahead to eavesdrop, and watched with a frown when the bus driver drew an S-shape through the air, the best route to take.

Mildred was telling us she was feeling the heat, and Ralph, who was driving their car, was not at ease with the idea of driving through the water. But Bergur had done it all before.

'Well,' Bergur asked, 'tell me, Ralph, do you have any experience driving across rivers?'

'Oh no, nothing to speak of. You think it'll be okay?'

'Yes, yes, I'm sure. It's not at all difficult. Of course, there are a few things you have to think about.' He took a moment to gather his thoughts together. 'Quite often, the rocks underneath the truck will slip. This can upset the truck's hold and make it more likely to tip.'

'Gosh.'

'Naturally, once the truck is off-balance, it'll be carried by the current. It's hard to know what to do when that happens. The truck may just get out, or you might just end up in the next underground lake.' This, I sensed, was a joke. 'Be especially careful about braking. And you'll find gear changes tricky. Don't let the speed of the current worry you. Take the crossing very slowly, and if you feel you're slipping, don't jerk the truck.' And with that Bergur got into his truck to move on.

The bus crossed first and two other four-wheel drives in front of us followed its trail of silver water, and then Bergur crunched his gears. We slipped and shuddered, and then crossed rather gently over the face of the smooth rocks beneath us. Bergur didn't check to see if the others had made it, having already resumed his story about milk deliveries in the pre-war years, but I turned around in time to see the rigid face of our Canadian telecommunications expert, who felt he had been thrown into a fight with a glacier, re-emerge with a smile.

Low clouds had gathered around the mountains when we came into Thórsmörk, so it was like we were entering a vast hall. A short walk would take us up to its ceiling, but Bergur and Mildred waited below. Mildred had at least discovered the source of all that heat, the car's bum warmer had been left on.

'It wasn't me, after all,' she said with relief. But she felt she was too old to make the trek. Bergur, for his part, said that he hadn't come all this way just to enjoy himself, and once again feigned a despair that had accompanied his humour of suffering and self-sacrifice since Mum had first met him thirty years before.

The summit was only half-an-hour's climb away, but even that brief ascent allowed us entry onto a roof of dark rocks covered in a crystal spray from the afternoon showers that had followed us into the valley. When we got back down, Bergur declared, 'The next stop is for us, Kári: Hlíðarendi.' Apparently, it wasn't that far away. We took the road inland to the other side of Markarfljót, a wide floor of glacial stones and streams. Out of it emerged the slopes of Hlíðarendi, the ones that had so moved Gunnar a thousand years before.

They were as fair and golden as the saga had promised, and I had to catch my breath at the sight of them. It was our last stop of the day, and although we had encountered some of the most beautiful landscapes of the south, I felt that it was only now, with the old stories as companions, that we truly saw Iceland. Stories made the landscape real, and added to the poet's light an energy that was as palpable to me as the energy that lay beneath the hot springs of the valley we had just left.

Ralph and I walked past the modern farm and a small church close by. Gunnar's farm, Bergur had told us, must have lain a little further up. As we reached the flat spot that Bergur thought was a possible site for it, Ralph and I sat down on a large stone and watched the others milling around the church below. In an adjoining field, a farmer and his daughter jumped a fence and walked even further up the slope. They were followed by a bounding dog that had found its own, rather long way around the fence. The clouds cleared over Eyjafjallajökull, revealing it as a white coat of snow.

As we sat looking out over the landscape, Ralph asked me about the story behind the place. I stressed Gunnar's sudden conviction to stay in Iceland, and how Gunnar's decision to stay had disappointed his closest friend, Njál, and his brother, Kolskeg, but had delighted his wife Hallgerð.

'But you're on his side, right?' asked Ralph. 'You think he did the right thing staying?'

'Oh, yes, definitely. Njál was a lawyer. His was a lawyer's advice.'

'But it would have saved his life.'

'The good thing about being a Viking,' I replied, 'was the afterlife. Gunnar was buried in a mound nearby. But he wouldn't sit still. He bothered the district for ages.'

'We don't get that option anymore, do we?' said Ralph.

I wasn't so sure. I rather hoped we did—wasn't that why I was here again, to see if I could have another go at bothering the district?

13

FAMILY NAMES

'So you're little Kári,' said my namesake, big Kári. He'd just returned from his summer holidays, very brown and not all that pleased to be back.

'You're not so little anymore,' he went on to observe. We were in the kitchen. I was cooking an omelette for dinner, and he stood close to the pan.

'Has my father been boring you with his stories, yet?' he asked.

'Yes, relentlessly,' I replied. 'But I'm a very willing victim.'

'Just don't mention the sagas. And please don't listen to any more of his stories. He won't stop if you do.' Kári took out a ladle and began to stir my omelette.

'I'll take you for a drive. There's more to Iceland than where Begur Jónsson first milked a cow.' He suggested a second trip to Thingvellir, probably towards the end of the week, when he'd have caught up with his backlog of tasks at the family company Skórinn, where he worked with Bergur and, presumably, had heard many stories about the old days on the farms.

It would be the first of many drives that the two of us would take there and, even now, more than ten years on, whenever I am in Iceland we drive there together. With each trip I become more addicted to the place, and more familiar with the smaller spaces that open up alongside the major faults in the earth. On that visit in 1999, I began to think I understood why the settlers had chosen it as their first parliament. It was a liberating landscape, but also sheltered. You walked from the windless bends of the river up to the top of the ridge, where the view expanded to take in the lake and a wide stadium of mountains. The combination of intimate, damp groves and wide, geological expanses created calmness, at least in me.

In a strange sort of way, it was the same at Bergur and Rut's. Their house was a collection of very intimate rooms around the enormous living area upstairs, which looked over the sea. Maybe that's what all great houses did, offered a contrast between closed and expansive space, and allowed the thoughts you had in each room to refine or expand the ones you had in others. But it was a first for me—I had never lived in a house big enough to have contrasts, moods.

Bergur and Rut were happy to take me in, and in tipsier moments would speak of me as one of their own. But in gentle ways they also demanded that I contact my family. They asked me who my father was, and I told them. From then on, Rut would remind me, even pointing at the calendar to reiterate it, that another week in Iceland had passed without me being in touch with Gísli. Bergur, meanwhile, was discretely asking around about Gísli and his connections.

'You must tell me when to stop,' he said. 'I don't want to look into this any more than you want me to.'

All I could think about was how lucky I was to be guided in this way. He didn't know my father himself, but had heard of my family and its ancestral farm, *Mýrarhús*, or 'Marsh House'. It was, he explained, a Reykjavík family with plenty of well-known descendants, including my Uncle Björn, who now lived and worked in Paris, and my Uncle Pétur, who had apparently been something of a character about town during his youth.

'Of course, it doesn't mean anything to be well-known in Reykjavík,' Bergur added.

Bergur and Rut said I should call Pétur. He would know my father's situation better than we could discover from a distance, even in Reykjavík. I agreed and was, I could see, perilously close to actually doing something about it. But still I waited and waited. Rut would again remind me that the days were passing by, and Bergur told me again that he wouldn't be able to find out much more on his own. And I really think that, if I had asked them, they would have made the phone call for me.

At long last, in the first week of September, I picked up the phone and called Pétur. He said he wanted to see me straight away.

'How long have you been in Iceland?' he asked.

'Just over a month.'

'And you haven't called until now!'

'Yes, I know, but I've been very busy at the university.'

'But we are family, Kári. You must always call your family when you first arrive.'

I offered my work as an excuse, but I was perplexed. How on earth was I to know I could ring?

Never mind, he'd said, telling me he'd meet me in an hour near the church at Seltjarnarnes. This worried me. Nine years on from meeting Gísli in the car yard, I wondered if I was in for another of those secret meetings.

I left a note for Bergur and Rut on the kitchen bench, saying I was going out to see Pétur and might not be home for dinner. I'd never left a note for them before, and I don't know what made me write one, then. I suppose I was apprehensive about meeting Pétur, afraid even of what might eventuate.

The sun was shining and, as I had an hour to get there, I decided to walk. I followed the length of the bike path to rows of new apartment blocks, where the atmosphere was suddenly suburban, with its typical emptiness of a weekday. There were few other pedestrians, and I must have been visible to Pétur for some time before I saw him. If I'd known that, I might have approached from the side, such were my nerves that afternoon.

He was leaning against a railing at the top of a small hill near a church. He was smiling, calling me over. He threw out his arms and pulled me in for a long hug. It was forceful, and consisted in good part of bristles and his woollen jumper. But there was no doubting it. He was delighted to see me.

'I could tell it was you,' he yelled close to my ear. 'You look just like us!' He had a point. Before me, was another version of my dipping chin, puffy cheeks, slight mouth.

'Don't you like this weather?' he asked. And, before I replied, 'You don't get good wind like this in Australia. This freshness! This is why you live in the North, Kári! Come on, let's go and talk.' He grabbed my shoulders and drew me towards the church. 'My house is just over there, on your family's old land. We'll find a spot in the sun.'

We left the road for a path that ran through plush lines of quiet homes, and then cut down to his street. Most of all, he seemed to want to show me his garden. So we spent quite some time looking at potatoes and other cold-weather vegetables. I didn't mind, but I didn't understand. It was as though I'd just seen him the summer before and he wanted to show me how the garden was coming along. Eventually, we settled down onto a thin, wooden bench.

'We can take in the sun here,' he said. 'Better to be outside, don't you think?' Again, I wondered why. Didn't he want me inside his house? I guess my thoughts reflected my preparedness for an offence of some kind.

'Are you back for good?' he asked.

When I told him that I was leaving in a few weeks, he again chastised me for not calling earlier. I felt a petty impulse to ask Pétur why he hadn't called us during the last twenty-seven years, but thankfully didn't say anything of the kind. He was as much an outsider to me as I was to him; he had probably thought it best not to ring.

'You know, I was always happy for your mother to say you were mine. It would've made things much easier for her.'

'Yes, Mum's told me that you wanted to help,' I replied.

'But she was too proud for that. Too proud to really accept help.' I wasn't so sure.

'I don't think Mum was ever proud. She has said that she

was, but I think it just felt easier on her own. Easier to cope with the disappointments.'

'But she shouldn't have denied herself the help. If only she'd told social services. No-one else needed to know.'

But I agreed with Mum on this one: the whole town would've known in a week if she had.

'Never mind,' continued Pétur, 'Let's go inside. I want to show you some things.'

So we went inside. Pétur, it seemed to me now, had just liked being outside when the weather was fine. It wasn't comp-licated at all, and I had no reason to think otherwise. He brought out a book-length genealogy of the family.

'Have a look through that while I make us lunch.' It was my family tree, but of course it was pointedly not mine as well. It contained no record of me. And yet as I leafed through it, I also recognised that with the help of relatives like Pétur, it would be easy enough to work out my ancestry and, in my own mind at least, insert myself into the record. Perhaps that was enough. Did anyone else need to know that there was a name missing, or that one of the missing names was mine? I'm sure there were hundreds like me, other illegitimate children who had miraculously evaded the totality of the Icelandic records system. Did they also think endlessly about who they were, and what was missing? Did they relate parenthood and home in the way I did?

Pétur asked what I'd be doing during the final weeks of my stay, and I confessed that what I wanted most was to meet my sisters and my brother. That was understandable, he said.

'They are your family. You should know them.'

'I hope it's not too late. It will be hard for them to suddenly meet a new brother,' I said. He then proceeded to give me a short history of each of my siblings.

Fríða Kristín was the oldest, and had just returned from many years in Spain. She was expecting her second child, due any day. She'd run away from home when she was sixteen to study art, and after that had gone into modelling. Anna, the second eldest, lived in the nearby village of Hveragerði, and from Pétur's description seemed to run half its businesses: the travel agency, the pizza shop and, yes, even a hot springs amusement park. Bryndís, the youngest of the girls, was living in Paris, had also worked as a model, and was now also expecting a second child, due any day. My two brothers, he continued, were called Björn and Ólafur. Yes, it was true, Ólafur had died young. But Björn was well and had just had his first child, Kristín, the middle name of both my eldest sister and grandmother.

Pétur said that each generation replicated something from the past, but of all the children only Björn was the settled type— he had gone into my father's business importing hardware and industrial equipment. The rest, he said, were wanderers, with Fríða and Bryndís being particularly stricken with the curse.

It was also true that Gísli's business had gone broke, and that he was unwell, just as we'd heard.

'Can you help me get in touch with them?' I asked.

'That wouldn't be quite right,' he answered.

'I'm not sure that I can do it on my own.'

'It is that kind of job, though. I don't see them very often. I can't really say that Gísli's family is very close to mine.' I watched him as he cooked. He must have felt my eyes on his back and turned around.

'I couldn't do it to your father. It would hurt him too much. I can't do that to my brother.'

There it was, I thought. We'd reached the point where the secret had started. That it was always about doing something to Gísli.

'I should take you for a drive,' said Pétur after lunch. Was this all anyone ever did, I thought, go for drives?

'I want to show you your Uncle Björn's latest project. He still does a lot of projects in Reykjavík.' I wasn't sure of his motives; I wondered if he was trying to get me out of the house before Bára, his wife, came home. We drove to a small, dark beach.

'You must remember this place from when you were a boy. You must have come down here from time to time.' In fact, it wasn't far from where Gunnar had kept his fishing tug during the winters. Across the water stood a cluster of apartment blocks on a thin strip of land. These, said Pétur, were his brother Björn's designs.

'And that's where your father lives,' he added, pointing across the water. So now I understood why we were here.

'You know,' he went on, 'if you wanted to, you could adopt the family name. It is Ólafs. A good, strong name! No-one would know whose you were, but you'd still be part of the family.'

He meant well. But without knowing it Pétur was replicating my own way, and looking for a solution that didn't really change anything, just so that Gísli would remain protected.

Pétur wanted me in, and at the same time he was as careful as I had been in saving his brother. Was a half-declaration of paternity going to be enough for me now? Was I to spend the rest of my life satisfied with this, a slightly better lie than the one I'd had before?

'Kári Ólafs,' he said. 'That has a good sound to it. You can even say that you're mine.'

'Kári Gíslason,' I replied. 'Pétur, I am Kári Gíslason. I am not anyone else's son.'

'Yes,' he said, 'that's true.' He looked at me hard once more, as though to confirm that it was time to stop, and said, 'Let's go for coffee, then.'

We went to Café Paris, where rather publicly he embraced and kissed me, and demanded that we be friends on our own terms, no matter what happened with Gísli. He asked if I felt like coming for a family dinner on Sunday?

'Yes, of course,' I replied. And with that, he kissed me again and let me on my way.

14

LETTERS TO ICELAND

There were no horses in Reykjavík that September, or at least none to throw me and bring on a decision, to shake me out of my rigidity and slowness. Perhaps you needed to be more like Gunnar of Hlíðarendi for that to happen, to be able to jump as far backwards as you could forwards, yet he too had doubts. He once asked his brother why he found it more difficult to kill than other men did. Even Gunnar, who was all action, occasionally permitted himself a moment of reflection—not a typically Viking thing to do.

I was the other way around, all reflection and not enough action. And so instead of leaping over an axe, I made myself a deal, one that I could manage without any horses, hard women, or even a thirst for vengeance. I would simply do what I had always done; I would write. Words ran parallel and, to some extent, removed from the real world; often they were just shapes on a page, as I had discovered at Mostyn House and in the sagas, when Egil locked himself away to die. They are another room for you to occupy. I would write a letter to my father and my siblings, and reach them that way.

In deference to the situation, I would write to Gísli first. He might want a chance to speak to Ólöf, his wife, before I contacted my siblings, and even though returning to Iceland wasn't about him anymore, I couldn't leave him out completely. It wouldn't be fair, especially as I was about to go back on a promise I had made, that he still had every reason to rely on. I wrote him a short note.

September 6, 1999

Gísli,

I arrived in Iceland on August 8. I would like you to know that I am going to be open about the fact that you are my father. This is a secret that should never have been created. It was very wrong of you to keep me hidden, and I will not live in secret anymore.

Kári

His apartment was so new that it didn't have a proper postal address yet, and I figured it would be better to deliver the letter in person. This rather undid the fantasy of my words carrying themselves and me, as I would have to carry them. What if I bumped into Gísli, or, worse still, his wife?

I had been slow to call Anna, Gunnar and Lilja's daughter, and her husband, Hreinn. I suddenly felt the oversight and phoned her on the day I wrote Gísli a letter. They invited me to see

Gunnar and Lilja's graves, and I decided the best thing would be to see them first, and then catch a bus to somewhere near Gísli's place. If I still felt like delivering the letter after visiting Gunnar and Lilja, I would pop it under his door.

We agreed to meet for coffee first, and then drive up to see Gunnar and Lilja.

'They were so happy that they knew you both,' said Anna. 'They hadn't known any foreigners before they met your mother. You and Susan were very important to them.'

I didn't doubt what Anna was saying—we had always felt the same way about Gunnar and Lilja—but I found myself wondering, yet again, why people had always been drawn to my mother and me in this way? Why did she bring out this generosity in others, and such willingness on their part to take us into their families? That was where our conversation drifted, and so it didn't seem altogether strange to tell Anna and Hreinn what I was planning to do that day, about the letter in my pocket.

'You must contact your siblings,' said Hreinn. 'You have to know your family. Your father and his wife will come around, I'm sure.' Anna was less certain. She looked worried, whether for me or Ólöf I'm not sure.

'Well, in any case, let's go visit Mum and Dad,' she said. 'They might well have the answers.'

They did, in fact, because they had never judged us. It wouldn't even have occurred to them to think less of us, or my circumstances, or our wanderings, or for us not insisting on help from Gísli. They were too happy with each other to even begin finding fault in others; it was a way of being that

I wanted as my own. They were the only people I have ever known who hadn't wanted to make an impression on others, who hadn't sought to be noticed. But how were you to remain unnoticed when it felt so close to being unknown?

As I stood before their graves their response came to me: 'Try not to judge your mother and father. Try to work out what you want, Kári. It isn't about finding someone to blame.'

'I just want to be home,' I replied.

'Þú ert heima, Kári minn,' Gunnar said. 'You are home, dear Kári.'

I caught the bus to near Gísli's apartment and walked the last bit down a long hill. Inside the apartment block stood a large pot, presumably to be used for plants one day, but now it was filled with odd bits of decorator's rubbish and quite a few letters, the strays of a new apartment block. None were addressed to Gísli and for a moment I wondered whether I was in the right place. But I didn't want to linger and look. I couldn't shake the unpleasant vision of the door opening, and of finding myself delivering the letter in person. I slipped it under his door, and almost ran down the stairs and out of the block.

It was a beautiful Icelandic afternoon, raining quite heavily and very windy—classic early autumn weather. I could barely hear myself yelling above the sound of the wind and the traffic coming down the hill. But I was yelling, euphorically in fact, and it was because I had finally done what I had been rehearsing for since I was seventeen. I was at last free of that drive to the president's lodge, when I had last been this close to my father.

⋖═══╡

That night, I wrote to my siblings. I had decided that I would post these letters the following day, so that they would reach my siblings two days after I had hand delivered the letter to Gísli. I feared that he might spoil things for me in the meantime if I didn't act quickly, but I was still glad I had at least allowed him some time. He had never told me to keep his secret— he had only ever asked—and giving him these two days was, I reasoned, my acknowledgment of the choice he had given me; now it was his chance to choose. I wrote a longer letter to my half-sister, Fríða, and similar ones to my other brother and sisters.

September 7, 1999

Dear Fríða,

I'm not sure if Gísli has ever told you about me, but I am Gísli's son and your half-brother. I was born in Reykjavík in 1972, my mother's name is Susan Reid, and since 1982 I have lived overseas; in England until 1986 and in Australia until today.

I am now visiting Iceland to do some research for my doctoral thesis. While I am here, I would very much like to meet my relatives, especially my sisters and brother, and my grandmother Fríða.

I met with my Uncle Pétur on Friday, and I had a lovely

dinner with Pétur, Bára, Ásdís and Kristján on Sunday night. I have also written to your brother and sisters—the same letter as this one to you.

I would like you to know that I have not written to you in order to cause any pain for you or your family. My reason for writing is simply that it would give me a great deal of pleasure to meet and know you.

I have already written to Gísli and told him that I don't want to live as a secret anymore.

If you would like to meet, perhaps you could call the number above after six pm and we can organise something. You are most welcome to meet me at Skildinganes, or we can meet at Pétur's house, or I can visit you.

I hope to hear from you soon.

All my best,

Kári

Reading these letters today brings back all of the excitement and apprehension of those three days, now more than ten years ago, when I waited to receive a reply. Today, I am embarrassed by the melodrama of my letter to Gísli. But it reminds me, as it should, that I was still very angry, and that my letter to him was more than just a hint for him to talk to his family. I judged him, and in retrospect I think I judged him too harshly.

Nine years before, he had told me that he loved my mother, and at the time that seemed enough. Between then and my letter to him, I had somehow come to think that it wasn't, and that I was entitled to blame him for a promise that my mother and I had made. My siblings, who at last come into this story in their own right, have since helped me move closer to my seventeen-year-old self. But partly that's because I had finally given up on Gísli acknowledging me.

At the time I wrote my letters, it seemed impossible that the response of my siblings would be altogether good, and their first contact still strikes me as a kind of miracle. How they managed such openness and warmth, which from the very beginning was their answer to the fact of my existence, I cannot imagine. Quite simply, they astounded me.

Fríða, the oldest, rang me on the very day their letters arrived. She introduced herself, and thanked me for writing, and then said that she'd just called Bryndís in Paris to tell her about me. Bryndís, she added, had just given birth to her second daughter, Opal.

'I've sent Bryndís a letter as well,' I replied, hastily. 'She'll get it soon, I expect.'

'Yes, I'm sure. That's fine, of course. And I've talked to Pétur as well. He has said that it's true. But *Pabbi*, our father, won't admit it. We have asked him, and he says he doesn't know you. He denies it completely.'

'I can understand Gísli saying that. I thought he might. It's been a secret a long time,' I said, pleased that Pétur had come through for me again.

'A very long time. You are twenty-six? A grown man?'

'Yes.'

'And your mother?'

'She is English. She worked with Gísli at G. Thorsteinsson & Jónsson.'

'Okay. We can talk more about that later. I've spoken to the others, and we all think it would be a good idea to meet. We really need to meet you for ourselves.' So we agreed that Agi, Anna's husband, would fetch me in an hour.

For a long time, I had felt myself suspended above the secret of my own identity. But when I came down I found that I had a lot to like about the world around me. Suddenly, I had a whole family that had in a way always been there. That night I even began to like my story, because it was obvious that it had led to this moment.

'How are they coping with the news?' I asked Agi, as we drove along the sea.

'I won't say they're not surprised, Kári. They can't quite believe that it's been kept a secret all these years. I mean, how did he do it? But I think they're fine. Or, will be. They've talked. They're very strong, very close. Your father raised beautiful children.' He smiled at me, and added, 'With some help, of course.'

'But he hasn't admitted it?'

'No, not yet. But he will have to. It's ridiculous.'

'You think?'

'Has no-one ever mentioned the resemblance to you before?'

'Well, my mother—quite a few times. She often says that I'm my father's son.'

'Yes, it's astonishing.' Agi smiled again and then turned off Suðurgata and began the descent to downtown. He had the most welcoming smile I'd ever seen, and behind it the mysterious warmth of regret. 'It'll be alright,' he continued. 'My family's just gone through something like this. I met a brother I'd never known. He died just after we met, actually.'

'Oh, dear. That's terrible.'

'No, no, it wasn't. The great thing was that we all got to meet.' Yes, I could see that, but I didn't want to repeat the sad outcome of Agi's half-brother; it would be nicer to survive well beyond the meeting, to have time to get to know them.

We stopped at an apartment block near Hlemmur, the bus terminus.

'C'mon, we'll go up,' said Agi, with the same, even happiness he'd used to calm me in the car. We wound our way through a narrow stairwell to an attic apartment, Fríða's place.

'Oh my goodness,' said Fríða, when she opened the door. She looked at the others.

'Yes, I know,' said Agi. 'I had a feeling you would say that.'

'Oh, *Pabbi*!' said Anna. 'Does he think we're blind?'

'What's wrong?' I asked, worried by their reaction.

'Don't worry. They are just a little in shock,' Björn said as they surrounded me, and passed me round for hugs and kisses.

'Is there really any doubt?' Fríða asked.

Poor Gísli, he had been right all along. It was, after all, the likeness that undid him. And that, as far as they were concerned, was that. There was nothing to do now but get to know me, and they have never since wavered in that first welcome, when they made their own decision about who I was, and what to do about me. If I was their brother, then I was their brother. There was nothing else to say.

There was a lot they wanted to know. How long was Gísli seeing my mother? How did she and Gísli meet? What sort of relationship did they have? Who else knew about it? Surely lots of people were in on the secret. Did he visit us, did he know me?

What do I remember of my responses to them? Mainly, that I didn't deny them anything they wanted to know. The information flooded out of me in a way that it could only do after so many years of keeping it in. I wanted it out, and all the more for it to finally come home to where it had always belonged.

Fríða brought out some photo albums and walked me through her own complicated life of relationships, migrations, and returns. Did I have any old pictures of me I could show them?

'No, I haven't brought any,' I said. I hesitated, and added, 'I'm sure I could send some.'

'Send them? You must bring them,' said Agi. He was busy taking his own photographs. 'Yes. Are you free on Sunday? We'll have lunch at our place in Hveragerði. We'll pick you up.'

'And this time we are bringing Gísli,' added Fríða. 'It's time he saw you.'

15

NEW ARRIVALS

I was surprised to find that Ólöf, my father's wife, also came to dinner. I could see that she hadn't slept much, and that her eyes were swollen from crying—it was still but a few days since she discovered that her husband had another child. But like the others there, she greeted me with a kiss and a hug and said, 'You're most welcome, Kári. Welcome to the family.'

It was a remarkable moment of self-possession and generosity, one which over the years she has drawn back from and eventually come to repeat. My sisters and my brother have never looked back: from the day they first met me, and in the face of intense pressure from both Gísli and Ólöf, they have stayed true to me and the feeling of familiarity and closeness from our first encounter.

These are generous people, and I have no trouble conceding that Gísli has played a part in shaping such a wonderful family. On that day, their first family dinner to include me, there was a very present love and respect for Gísli, even with the upheaval of the previous few days. He wasn't very well, even though his Parkinson's disease wasn't at an advanced stage yet, and he looked drawn and tired, much older than a man who had only recently turned sixty. The resemblance between us had all but gone; it would, I now realised, only be seen by someone who'd known him as a young man, when he had met my mother.

I see now that I was coming into the family as he was beginning to leave it. In the years to come, he would become more ill and less able to cope with any mention of either me or my mother. His explanation for me would change—I was the product of a one-night stand, a brief affair at work—and I don't believe he ever admitted the whole story.

That day, he was as generous in spirit to me as the others were to him. He shook my hand warmly and said he was pleased to see me. He made no reference to the letter, although I found out later that he had received it—it hadn't ended up in the pile of uncollected mail in the flower pot.

Fríða drew me aside, most concerned that I should have a long talk to him. She manoeuvred us into armchairs in the centre of the living room and then, not-so-subtly, organised for herself and Anna to hover and listen in. It was set-up rather like a chat show, and probably not conducive to an intimate exchange.

'How did you break your nose?' he asked.

'I fell over, as a kid.'

'I don't remember your mother mentioning that. And what do you do now?' he asked.

'I'm in literary studies.'

'Yes, that makes sense.'

'Why so?' I thought someone was, at last, going to shed some light on my choices in life.

'Well, you know you're a descendant of Snorri's.'

'No. Snorri who?'

'Snorri Sturluson, of course.'

Of course. The saga author. The one who died in 1241.

'You're mother chose a beautiful name,' he continued. 'But how do they say it in Australia?'

'There's a girl's name that's spelt the same. They call me that.' I pronounced it for him.

'But your "a" has an accent.'

'Yes, but I don't insist on it.'

'You should. You should be proud of your Icelandic name. Say it as we say it here. How is your mother? Is she here as well?'

'No, she's in Brisbane. She's well. Still working.'

'Will you pass on my best?'

She had always said I was just like my father, but all the same I doubted that this was the conversation that I would have had with a long-lost son. A broken nose, a famous Icelandic ancestor, the correct pronunciation of a name, and greetings to a lover from years ago. We were different. I was both less outwardly assured and more openly sentimental than Gísli. I would have searched for a common soul from the very first meeting, however absurd that might have seemed. I would have wanted to know him. But I couldn't fault Gísli's behaviour towards me that day. Now that the past had caught up with him, he took the consequences blithely, perhaps even nonchalantly. It was a reaction that could well have annoyed a wife;

he was probably relieved, and I sensed that he rather enjoyed himself that day.

All the same, I sensed that I had to be content that our relationship might end here, and that we were still no closer to becoming father and son in any meaningful sense. Had he been a different man—more emotional, less protective of his position—I would maybe still be looking for him, and for something that might develop alongside the warmth shown by my siblings. But it was too late for that. He was ill, and it was an illness that made him even more hesitant than before, if not exactly about me anymore. The secret was over, but the fear that it had once produced was remaindered in his manners and his health. As with our meeting at the president's lodge, I was in no doubt that this was not the start of something.

Perhaps, this sense of it all having come too late was how my mother had felt when I was five and she left him for Australia. She had moved him out of the picture and concentrated instead on earlier desires: the intense longing for Iceland, the restlessness that had predated him.

Over the course of the dinner, Fríða's contractions had become more regular and intense, and she began to time them. It was a day for new arrivals, Agi said: a baby and a twenty-six-year-old love child. At eight, we drove back over the high ground between Hveragerði and Reykjavík. It was a cold, clear evening, and as we came down off the heath the northern lights began to trace their way towards town. Fríða sat in the front passenger seat puffing lightly. The next day, she gave birth to her second child, a boy.

When I got to Bergur and Rut's, I called Mum. I had been waiting until after the gathering, and until I knew how things would go with Gísli and Ólöf. It was noon in Australia, a bright September day, said Mum, the best time of year in Brisbane. There would have been gentle sunshine and a breeze brushing through the apartment. We talked for over an hour—mostly, she wanted to know about Gísli's family—she actually knew very little about them, and had long wanted to know more. In a way, my siblings had been kept a secret from my mother and me, too. He had divided his world so well, each part sheltered from the other.

I joked about my being related to Snorri Sturluson.

'Well, it was always the finest of everything with Gísli,' she said.

'Including you, Mum?' I asked.

'Well, I suppose I must have had something about me,' she replied.

I also rang Ólöf to ask if we could meet again. I wanted to see her before I left Iceland, partly because I liked her and thought, perhaps naively, that she and I could get along, despite everything, and partly because I feared she would stop my siblings from seeing me. I was, in a way, right about both things. Yes, she had liked me that Sunday afternoon and, no, it was nothing against me in particular but she couldn't see me again. That was impossible. And over the days that followed, the news filtered through to me that she'd asked Fríða and the others to stop seeing me, too. Thankfully, without success.

It now seemed like there was no time left at all until I had to return to Brisbane but I had twenty-six years to catch up on with my siblings, so I spent less time at the saga institute. I was being drawn in—into Iceland and out of myself—and out of what suddenly seemed an exaggerated sense of isolation, dwelt upon until it became everything. Perhaps that was the lesson of my life: you were never as far from being included as you thought you were.

After work one evening, Fríða and I met at her place and went for a walk down Laugavegur, the main street. We were going visit to Amma Fríða, our grandmother, who still lived in the same house in Bárugata as when Mum and Gísli had walked past it nearly thirty years before.

Inside, the house was every bit an expression of the history and, indeed, the size of its occupant. Nowhere was this more evident than on the top floor, where her sofas and pictures nestled under a sloping ceiling that was an ideal height for her but must have been awkward for her sons. Maybe that was the plan, in order to keep it for herself. It was where she wanted to sit down and, she said, talk to me properly for the first time.

In this house, she told me, she had raised three boys to be successful and confident, but in their own ways each was a little reckless too. Perhaps, I thought, this was because they'd grown up without a father, like me. It might also have been because they had grown up to be slim, handsome boys with thick hair and light smiles from a passing world, the old Iceland. As they became young men, the softness of youth had been replaced by a charm that may have been invisible to some—at least until you got to know them better—but which I saw plainly enough in the photographs that Amma Fríða brought out.

'You can see why he was popular,' she said.

She made us coffee. One of her thin, pale hands held mine, and with the other she patted my face.

'You're most welcome in my house,' she said. There wasn't even the slightest hint of unease about who I was; I could have been holding Lilja's hand. Perhaps this was the spirit of the women of her generation. Perhaps she was simply a kind mother who understood her sons too well to judge the results of their errant ways. Or, I wondered, maybe when she saw me, she was reminded of my father as a younger man, someone else who hadn't known his father.

'I don't think I've got too much longer left,' she said. 'I'm glad you came when you did.'

'It's lucky for me, then. I took my time, I suppose.'

'Very rude of you,' she said. 'Your manners are getting better now, though.'

I couldn't help but wonder whether Gísli's fear of upsetting Ólöf had originated in this room, with a fear of his mother's loneliness? But I quickly told myself to stop thinking about him, and in the next moment looked again at the photograph. Maybe he just didn't like getting caught. And, then again, maybe he did.

My grandmother Fríða Kristín died not long after I left Iceland. I was in Brisbane at the time and couldn't attend the funeral. Pétur, who at the funeral read out the list of surviving relatives, was particular in including my name among the grandchildren. The inclusion was among the first of many such acknowledgments that the Ólafs family had a new member, and more than ten years on I have no doubt that I am known in Iceland for who I really am: the son of an English woman and an Icelandic man who fell in love and, despite the difficulties of their relationship, stayed true to a promise they had made to each other.

There must come a moment for all parents when our children no longer completely accept our vision for them. I must remember that in the future, for breaking the promise to Gísli was the best thing I'd done in my life, and not merely because things worked out with my siblings. It allowed me to close a door on my father—despite his acceptance of what I'd done, I didn't want to see him again—and open a door on Iceland that I had long thought could only be opened by him. Could I return to Iceland when there was nothing in the way of my return?

When you write a story like this one, it is tempting to look for section breaks, places where the story pauses or takes on a different mood. I think they must be fairly obvious: the early impetus behind my story lay with my mother's love of Iceland, and her love affair there; there was my childhood in Reykjavík, one that set me up for my interminable nostalgia about the country; there was a separation, when we moved to England and then Brisbane where I rebuilt my Iceland out of the sagas; and now a return, when family, the landscape of Reykjavík, and its old stories met for the first time.

If it's true that you can discover yourself in writing the story of your life, you also lose some of the old certainties. Across section breaks emerge unsettling through lines. I had a growing awareness that over the years a deep anger had settled beside my hopes for Iceland—the search for love had brought with it a touch of hate. That October, as I boarded my plane to London and began the long series of flights that connect Reykjavík and Brisbane, I was aware that I still had another section break to write into my story. I wasn't quite home yet.

16

ISLANDS APART

If Reykjavík is the freshness of the North Atlantic wind, then Brisbane is all about liquid aroma—the heady comforts of the Pacific. When I stepped off the plane a month later into a November night, I welcomed the heavy fragrances of the coming summer. Strangely, for the first time it felt like home, or at least a home.

A friend picked me up from the airport and, on the way to my mother's apartment, I asked if we could stop by the river and take in the air for a moment. We pulled off the road at Toowong, a river suburb just outside the city, and breathed it in. It had taken a return to Iceland to recall just how enveloping the atmosphere here was. It picked you up and carried you away with the pollen.

When I got to Mum's, I pulled out a photo collage that my siblings had given me before I left Iceland. Its frame had been much too big for my carpetbag so Rut had taken me shopping for what must have been the largest suitcase in Reykjavík. Even with the bigger case the glass had broken. It was a familiar problem—how to bring awkward items from overseas to Australia. Mum's solution had always been not to even try. She would give away her furniture before each move, and start again. I was more attached to objects than she, more material. I thought that you could probably have a little bit of Reykjavík in Brisbane, even if the glass broke.

We spent the night looking over old photographs, hers as well as some that Fríða had given me, and there we began a process of bringing two islands closer together: our story and theirs, Iceland and Australia. It knows no end, because I can't ever place one island perfectly over the other. There is quite a difference in their size.

I soon raised the idea of changing my surname. Even though Mum was now long-since divorced from Ed, she hadn't changed her name back to Diggons. She was comfortable with Reid—it had eventually become how she thought of herself. But, for me, Reid remained a cover of sorts, a way around the patronymic. Oddly, although I didn't want Gísli any more, I did want his name.

For a while, I had been toying with the idea of using Gíslason as a middle name, but this struck me as a concession to the secret—hiding Gísli in the middle. No, it had to be the patronymic, just as it would have been had my situation been different. You couldn't rewrite history. But you could at least make minor corrections here and there.

The following year, in 2000, I changed my name and began to save for another ticket to Iceland.

It was busy in the branch, with people going everywhere. One of the travel agents was very beautiful, very blond and rather more energetic behind the counter than the others. She was direct, even a little blunt. When it was my turn, she said Reykjavík was no problem but she'd need to spend a day on it before she could give me a fixed itinerary. Could I come back tomorrow? Of course I could. When I turned to leave, she was walking behind the row of chairs to fetch brochures for the next customer. She wore a short grey skirt, black stockings, and a grey polo with purple bands on the arms.

The next day, I took a little extra care in my presentation. A close-fitting, ironed shirt. New jeans. Green shoes, even. Her blond hair was pushed back, and I thought I caught her taking me in. A German face, I thought now, a little Icelandic even.

'May I have a brochure, please?' I said.

'For Iceland?'

'If you have one.' And off she went along the row of travel agents, through to the brochures in the back office.

Some weeks passed, and then I had to go in to tell her I needed to push my departure back a little.

'How long will you stay in Iceland?' she asked idly.

'Six months this time.' She glanced back at the computer screen.

'We should be able to fix this.' Her arm was in a sling. 'Skiing,' she explained. 'I'm always doing this.'

'No more sport for a while, then.'

'No. Strictly indoor activities.'

I hadn't meant to pick French porn. There was nothing in the title of the film to say that it was French porn. And, in any case, we shouldn't be embarrassed about young people discovering their bodies. The French weren't.

She was driving an old Volvo sports hatchback; it was fifteen years old, the same age as the young people discovering their bodies. The car rattled, and the rubber lining on the hatch door squeaked. I liked that: it matched Gunnar's definition of a good, honest car—you could hear its parts.

After the film we drove to a local café, where we shared a piece of cheesecake.

'I've got a big day tomorrow,' she said. 'I should probably make a move. Do you need a lift somewhere?'

'Just to Mum's,' I said.

'Of course. You're still living with your mother.'

It was just while I was saving for Iceland, I explained, but I'm not sure that helped much. We followed Swann Road to Taringa. There was a pause, and then a look that all but pushed me out. There was no peck for the man who lived with his mother and took girls to pornos.

It was a terrible first date, but she saw her way past it. It was September 2000. Would I like to come to an Olympics party, she asked. A night of swimming on TV: thin men in swimwear, young people discovering their bodies in a much better way. Kieren Perkins was going to be making his exit from the sport. Parents would drop in. We could forget about the movie thing.

'So you're off to Iceland in three months,' Olanda said later that night at a club we'd found in Caxton Street.

'That's right,' I replied. 'I know we're only out dancing, but I guess that puts us in a funny position.'

'Only if we let it.'

'It doesn't worry you that I'll be leaving soon?'

'Not yet. I don't know how long I'll be in Brisbane, either.'

It was the line we held onto over the next three months: we wouldn't let it bother us, not yet. She was also unsure of her future—the reason she was a travel agent was that she wanted to travel. We just had to enjoy what we had while we had it.

On Boxing Day, I left for Reykjavík as planned, following the dawn across to London, and then up to Iceland. It was the forty-eight-hour day that I'd lived half-a-dozen times before. But this time I phoned Brisbane en route, from transit lounges in Sydney and then Singapore and London, and eventually from Bergur and Rut's place.

'All that stuff about taking things as they come,' I said, 'total rubbish. I'm not even sure why I'm in Iceland, anymore.'

'It's because you wanted to go,' she replied. 'You want to be there, remember.'

'But six months . . .'

'. . . is only six months.'

I began my work at the saga institute and found a student apartment. In a few weeks, Mum would be visiting. She was going to celebrate her sixtieth birthday party in Iceland; Bergur and Rut would host it at their place and I would cook. In the meantime, a long winter of storms and darkness began, which I attempted to break through with walks to the frozen phone booth on Suðurgata for conversations with Olanda in Brisbane, where she lay sweating under the fan.

'What was I thinking? I could be there with you.'

'Don't torture yourself like this,' she replied. 'Be patient.'

'It's ridiculous. I can't keep putting Iceland ahead of everything else.'

When I confided in my namesake big Kári that I was tortured by regret over leaving Olanda, he said that the only way to ward off my loneliness was to go for a drink. We headed into town, first to Dubliners and then to a sports bar, where TV screens behind the bar played porn, of all things. It was grim, and not at all the delicate French porn of my first date with Olanda. We sat across from each other with pints of dirty-tasting beer.

'To the single life!' I toasted. 'Isn't it grand?'

'Yes,' he replied, 'imagine if Olanda was here. I wouldn't get to drink with a loser who gave up a beautiful girlfriend in Australia to sit here with me and watch porn. You've definitely made the right choice.'

'Thank you. You understand me perfectly.'

'It must be good to get away from the beaches, the cheap food, the wine,' he continued.

'That's right. You can have too much of those things,' I replied.

'Well, you're okay now. You won't get any here, I promise. No fun until you leave.'

There was no denying that we were having a great time, but we eventually called it a night. Kári's apartment lay further up Laugavegur, mine towards the university, and we parted ways on Bankastræti, near a tatty-looking strip club. I looked through the door to a reception area of tall girls in miniskirts.

'Come in,' said one. 'Have a drink. Warm up.'

I kept walking, past Café Paris and across Austurvöllur, the town square, to a line of telephone booths on the other side. It was two in the morning, very cold, and dark in the way that only Iceland can be dark, as though it were a permanent state, as though the world of light would never be rejoined. A malicious wind wound through the office blocks.

'Hey, it's me,' I said into the phone.

'How was your night with Kári?' asked Olanda.

'Medium. I know just the spot to go if you ever want to watch porn with your beer.'

'Once was enough, thanks.'

In the years since my mother had left Iceland, the army of secretaries had splintered badly. Judith and Nanci had fallen out over promissory notes that Haukur had obtained before he died. Molly and Patricia were also at loggerheads over something, presumably animals and artwork, possibly Jersey as well. They were getting cranky in their old age, thought Mum. And crazier, too.

I asked Mum if she wanted to look up Gísli. She replied that she couldn't think of anything worse, but that she longed to meet my sisters.

They got along beautifully. Fríða and Bryndís had their share of restlessness, a thirst for the wider world. I was sure that, had the three of them met in the 1970s, they would have been friends; my mother had been taken to Iceland for the same reasons they had been taken away. The meeting was, in a way, the end of a long road for Mum—she wanted to apologise for the affair, and as she did so I was given a rare glimpse of just what a burden the secret had been, no doubt for both her and Gísli. How, I wondered, had she borne such anxiety for thirty years? How could you wait that long to say sorry?

There was no simple answer to either question, but more than ever I was convinced that she had loved him deeply, and that her desire to know my sisters was because they were his children, and not because they were my siblings. Meeting them brought her a step closer to his world, one that she hadn't been able to enter completely when she was with him. And while we may have moved to Australia to escape the affair—to finally end it, as she had told me—the meeting with my sisters confirmed to me that she never really had. In many respects, she was still there, in a wind-blown outpost of Europe in the 1970s.

While not all the secretaries made it to dinner on the night of Mum's sixtieth, there were enough there to recollect old time, which to some extent recreated the atmosphere of thirty years before. In the end, they didn't reminisce much, but the gossip and the laughter of the evening was a kind of reminisc-ing, enacted rather than verbalised. Bergur, now as then, tried to place himself at the head of a group that saw him as merely a lovable man whose much more important wife was provid-ing them with a place to meet. Were men ever capable of more than that, of being loved, included at dinner, and humoured when they tried to involve themselves in the affairs of the day?

I wanted to understand Mum and her relationship with the other women who'd fallen in love here. But the army always slipped a little beyond my grasp. Perhaps it was the constant gossiping that kept you out: keeping the conversations overloaded also left the evenings free from real analysis. Or was it their concern for me that ultimately made it impossible for me to really get them? For thirty years, they had been busy working me out, and in doing so had instructed me in self-analysis. They weren't quite ready for me to turn the lens on them.

Nor was Mum. I don't know if she saw it this way, but the night marked the thirtieth anniversary of the only time she and Gísli had gone out together, to the boat-shaped restaurant downtown. Tonight, Iceland was a different place, and also I suspect the same place that she had encountered when she first arrived: cold, windy, and difficult—the sort of place you came to for two years, not for a new life. And as we walked along Suðurgata the next day, she said that she didn't think she'd be able to cope with the winters again. From then on, she'd visit in summer, when life in Iceland turns out into the streets, the parks, and the countryside.

There was little sign of spring when Olanda arrived—we hadn't managed to be apart for six whole months. She joined me in March, when it was minus five, and a fine gale blew across town. There was nothing to do but stay indoors for a week. This went very well; she liked to sit on the broad windowsills of our apartment and watch the snowstorms drift along the narrow street. The midnight blue of dawn extended the nights, and when we finally emerged each day it was into a quiet noon barely touched by human activity.

We were only two steps from the haphazard urbanity that I so loved about Reykjavík. Our walks around town followed Fríkirkjuvegur, a street named after the Icelandic Free Church that lined the length of the pond and cornered towards a thawed section of water, where a gang of ducks and swans begged aggressively. Behind Fríkirkja, the dog-legged streets of Austurbær formed tiers for dark-coloured Mercedes and Audis. But on the long seashore strip, merchant and fishing life retained a hold. There were warehouses, trawler wharfs, dry docks, and crumbling stevedoring buildings.

In the evenings, before dinner, we caught the bus down to Laugardalslaug for a late swim. We would sit in the hot pot watching a small clock that hung nearby, calculating as precisely as we could the last minute to get out and still catch the bus to make our way back in to town.

We talked a lot about living in Iceland, and whether we could move there for good. Olanda wanted to try it, but already reservations showed in her eyes. The Icelanders unsettled her—they didn't smile, for one thing. Why was everyone always frowning? It wasn't exactly a frown, I explained, more a well-meaning glare, or just the villager's curiosity that survived into the modern era. If you believed the old travel writers, it was also peasant surliness, a leftover from the crofter years—they were the stares of malnutrition. But there were other, more benign remnants of the old style of life, too.

One evening, as Kári was driving us back to the university flat, he asked Olanda how she was getting along.

'Great,' she replied. 'It's beautiful. I'm sure I'll get to know more people the longer I'm here.'

'And you're all sorted in the apartment?' Kári continued.

'Yes, not too bad. If we can just get some music into the place, it'll be quite homely.'

The next morning we opened the door to a grinning Kári with a stereo still covered with the dust from his teenage years. It was hard to reconcile the hospitality of those you knew with the air of hostility that you often encountered on the streets but, for me, it was a familiar contrast, and one I didn't mind. Bumping into friends, which in Reykjavík you simply couldn't avoid, was always like coming in from the cold weather outside. Iceland was all about intimate circles that existed as a way of differentiating yourself within a small community. For Olanda, it didn't make any sense.

The reality is that Iceland only really works for people who fall hopelessly in love with it, and it was plain that hadn't happened for Olanda. But for the time being, we settled on looking for more, for the softness that undoubtedly lay beneath the brittle Icelandic exterior. It was for me to play the role of the guide, and although I doubted that I was as suited as my father had been thirty years before, I was sure it was possible. But then a crisis arose.

Olanda fell ill. One night when we had met some of my colleagues for a drink downtown, she began to burn with a fever and started to pass out. I rushed her home, and called for a doctor. It wasn't clear what was wrong, the doctor said. I was to keep an eye on her; by the morning, she would probably feel a little better. But the next day she could barely move and her lower back ached terribly. I rang Rut, who rushed us to the hospital. Olanda's temperature had climbed dangerously high, which at that point was the main concern. It then turned out she had a severe kidney infection, and she'd probably been carrying it for weeks.

The next morning, Olanda's condition had worsened. She'd reacted to the antibiotics the doctors had prescribed to control the infection—they made her even more ill than the infection. It was becoming harder for her body to control her temperature, and she was badly dehydrated.

'They say they've worked you out now,' I told her, when she finally came to under medication that suited her.

'At last, someone,' she replied.

I hadn't wanted to leave her side the whole time. The nurses said I could sleep on the couch in the visitor's lounge, even thought it wasn't really the done thing. When I looked for it the first night I found it made up with a pillow and a blanket.

On the third day of the crisis, Bergur and Rut and my sisters visited, and Olanda had begun to improve. She insisted that I get a lift home with Rut.

'At least have a shower,' she half-joked.

It is awful to be sick in a foreign country. Auden began a poem about Iceland with this line: 'And the traveller hopes: "Let me be far from any physician".' I say, let me be free of local emergency wards. Illness can change how you see the people around you, and Olanda began to view Bergur and Rut and my sisters, even the strangers around us, a little differently. It wasn't merely that they'd helped us, but that they loved Olanda. She also noticed that part of their concern was selfish: they wanted us to settle here.

A few days later, Bergur and Rut picked us up from the hospital. While the worst of the illness had passed, Olanda's full recovery took some weeks, and her enjoyment of the coming spring would be limited by the amount of time she could comfortably spend outside. She had seen how warm our circle of friends and relations could be, but she was also reminded of how far away her own family was, and how quickly that could matter. In May, we began to plan our return to Brisbane.

When we arrived back, we moved into a share house together. We bought bookshelves, and then a table, and then eventually our own apartment in Paddington, a suburb of steep hills and Queenslander homes just north of the city. Olanda went back to her job at STA Travel and I settled down to finish my doctorate about medieval Iceland. Reading about the Iceland of the far-distant past still offered a way back, but by starting to go back in person I also now understood that reading was merely the beginning of the journey home. I also now understood that the return couldn't be made on my own.

17

INTO THE FJORDS

The Iceland question was put off, but only for so long. Early in 2003, a German friend and colleague, Steffi, in whom I had often confided my longing to return, put me in touch with Ólina, a journalist and ethnographer from Ísafjörður, a town of three and a half thousand people in the remote Westfjords. Ólína had also been a politician and was now the principal at Ísafjörður Grammar School. After I received my doctorate in Brisbane late that year, I wrote to Ólína, asking if she would employ me as an English teacher.

If we needed a weekend out of Brisbane, Olanda and I would normally drive to Noosa on Queensland's Sunshine Coast. Locals made fun of it as being twee and more suited to trendy Melbournians than Queenslanders, but we liked the cafés, the calm Hastings Beach, and the sheltered coves and pandanus palms of Laguna Bay. Olanda's family had long since come there for holidays, and partly for that reason Noosa was chosen as the place to celebrate her grandparents' fiftieth wedding anniversary. It was September 2003.

It had been several years since I'd written a poem—it seems that I'd become a little too happy for that; certainly, it helped that the woman I loved also loved me. But while we were celebrating the anniversary, I found myself writing a poem about getting married, and one evening on the rocks that led from Hastings Beach to Little Cove I read it out loud to Olanda. It was sunset, her family was waiting for us at a restaurant nearby, and the sea was beginning to cool and colour in the sand around our feet. Even though I couldn't afford an engagement ring, what choice did she have but to say yes.

The following Australia Day, in 2004, we were married. We had a small, simple wedding on the rocks at Noosa. As the time for the ceremony approached, heavy clouds built up around the hills behind the beach. It was going to storm and just as Olanda came down the steps to the beachfront the storm hit, but we pressed ahead. Our wedding continued to the sound of thunder.

We exchanged our vows, kissed and then, of course, the storm cleared, which we took as a sign of something, either of our good fortune in being together or Godly relief that the service was over. The saga authors would have known which interpretation to make, but the Australian lifeguards mattered more that day. They had closed the rest of the beach but couldn't bring themselves to move our little party on. Later they told us that the umbrellas we were using were illuminated for the whole of the service; there had been a band of sunshine at the tail of the storm.

For me, the idea of a year in the Westfjords was appealing. It would take me beyond Reykjavík and towards what my father and most Icelanders saw as the other, more interesting Iceland of the farmlands and fishing villages: the outer extremes of the island, where the Icelandic character was, supposedly, distilled. Olanda liked the idea, too: she wanted to help me return, but she also needed to change things for herself. If nothing else, the Westfjords would be a change.

Bergur and Rut were not the first to express their misgivings— my mother, our friends in Brisbane, Olanda's parents, and my colleagues at the university all wondered what on earth I thought I was doing taking my new wife to a village in the Arctic Circle. But Bergur's father had been a merchant in Flateyri, a village in Önundarfjörður just to the south of where we were going, and so Bergur's questions were the most searching.

'In winter, there's no direct sunlight for weeks on end,' he said. 'Even on clear days, the sun doesn't make it over the mountains.'

'And what will Olanda do while you're teaching?' asked Rut.

I didn't answer. What did you do in a fishing town eight hours' drive from Reykjavík, closer to Greenland than Europe? Now and then, polar bears arrived there by sea ice. There was only so much entertainment to be gained from that.

Then, I said, 'I don't think the difference between Reykjavík and Isafjörður is as great for us as it is to you.'

'And I will get a chance to think about what I want to do next,' added Olanda.

What I really wanted to say was that I didn't care about

the practicality, because in the end it was all a little beyond my scope. I was here to chase something that I had been chasing for the last twenty years. There was nothing more uncertain than returning to the place where you thought you might belong. How was I meant to think about whether it would actually be enjoyable as well?

I didn't tell them that, not because I didn't trust Bergur and Rut with the truth, but because I was embarrassed to admit my hope of a homecoming and my belief that it would all fall into place. Instead, I laughed off their concerns and declared that Olanda and I would go seal hunting on the weekends. And, yes, I promised to find something horrible for her to do in the fish factories.

We landed in Ísafjörður on a clear afternoon in August, when winter couldn't have seemed any further away. The airport, a single strip tucked along the fjord's eastern side, was just a shed. But a ten-foot conveyor belt had been built through the wall, making the baggage claim more official looking. Behind the locals collecting their shopping from the baggage claim stood Guðni, the school caretaker, who said that he'd been sent by Ólína to take us up to the school.

It was mild outside, at least fifteen degrees Celsius; much warmer than we'd expected. The fjord was long and green, and patches of grass reached all the way up to its topmost ridges. I noticed that above the airport lay a large hollow in the mountains. My students would later tell me that trolls were the cause, and indeed it looked like a troll had made his seat there. Later that day, when I went up to the schoolrooms to introduce myself, I found that my office looked out across the spit to the hollow.

'You can climb up there,' said Guðbjartur, the deputy principal.

'I must,' I replied, 'seeing as my office faces it like this.'

He had been assigned the duty of giving me a tour of the school. He took me through the history of nearly every corridor and teaching room, each time adding something about what we were seeing through the windows. I think he was announcing his role in my life, which was less about guiding my teaching than introducing me to rural Iceland. He believed in details.

The next day, I met Rúnar, the sociology teacher who, like Guðbjartur, saw me as a prodigal son and wanted to make sure I felt at home. Both he and Guðbjartur were castaways, each looking for something new in the Westfjords, and perhaps that is why they wanted to help me. It was the sort of helpfulness I knew from before, from my mother's experiences and from my other returns, when the locals would demand that I come back for good. There is nothing you can do better in Iceland than like Iceland—if you share their intense fondness for the place, the locals will do just about anything to teach you why you love it so much.

There were obstacles, though. Very quickly it was clear that there wasn't going to be any work for Olanda, and my joke of sending her to the fish factories took on the look of a prophecy. The apartment we'd rented in advance of coming was in Tungudalur, a beautiful valley of summerhouses and forest walks, but hopelessly out of the way. It seemed that most of the people in the town were either school-aged or late middle-aged—our own age group was, I suppose, as in most remote towns, away either studying or making the better money on offer in Reykjavík. The beautiful isolation of the fjords was looking like it could also be a bit lonely.

Ólína's husband, Sigurður, who was writing a book about the town, said to me that in the 1980s the town had been a lively, but worn-looking place. What I now saw out of the staff-room windows was a very pretty version of Ísafjörður, but also the quietest it had ever been. As it turned out, only a cluster of old houses in the centre of the spit were pretty. Around them had been erected a Soviet fence of concrete houses and factory buildings, and the main street wound indecisively through some of them before crumbling into the sea.

It would always be the location of the town that was most stunning. Ísafjörður followed a spit out into the middle of the fjord, curving into a shipping lane of trawlers and small fishing boats. The calm side was still enough to be used by kayakers, but to the north the fjord opened towards the wild, abandoned mountains and valleys of the country's extreme north-west. Some of the richest fisheries lay just out there in those waters, but increasingly they were being harvested by companies from Reykjavík and Akureyri. Ísafjörður was in danger of becoming a museum town, a commemoration of the old days when fishermen had to live close by the fishing grounds.

My students, most of whom were in their last year at school, had no doubt about what lay ahead. They would reluctantly have to leave, probably for Reykjavík, which they regarded as the one truly vile town in Iceland. None shared my love of the late evening light in Vesturbær or over Mount Esja, which they joked was just a mound. But I understood their reluctance to leave the place they loved; it was the same as mine.

Olanda and I moved closer into the centre of town to a tiny basement apartment in a large house in Hjallavegur, or 'Slope Street'. The house was owned by the only other occupant, Alma, a widow who lived upstairs and worked in the local council. She told us we could keep our bikes in her late husband's workshop, still cluttered with his tools and half-finished projects. She'd have to do something about the workshop one day, she said. Upstairs, the rooms felt as unchanged as the garage. Very much a woman's space, full of framed photographs of grandchildren and holidays. Alma was originally from the East Fjords, but she didn't want to go back. This was home, I guessed because it had been their home together.

'I would never leave Ísafjörður,' she said, 'not now. This is a good town.' I wondered whether she was lonely, being so far from her family in the east. But they visited once or twice a year, and each summer she would go to them.

We had bought our bikes at a drastically reduced figure from their summer price—I was almost afraid to buy them. The sales assistant assured me, though, that there was nothing wrong with them; it was merely that some people didn't like riding in the winter. I taught in the mornings that semester, and Olanda and I spent the afternoons cycling, most often to Tungudalur, the same valley where we'd decided not to live, but which became our regular destination instead.

The valley took us past a small golf course and into a hillside forest of conifers and mossy groves. A steep stream ran from the heathlands above—the ridges dividing us and the next fjord to the south, forming a path of grey-blue movement through the berries and stone escarpments. We had a picnic table to ourselves that, along with a flag post, furnished a raised clearing. From there, we could see the plane from Reykjavík making its precarious final turn into the fjord, becoming minuscule against the soaring immensity of the mountain, the troll's seat, and the bluffs.

We once rode as far as Súðuvík, the village in the next fjord. It was a difficult ride, and took much longer than we'd expected. Passing cars threw up stones that caught our ankles, and the drivers rubber-necked as they sped by. But on the way back we had a long downhill stretch, and Olanda took off on her own, arms in the air. She wooed the whole way down the hill, a good kilometre in length.

'Slow down!' I called out, but she wouldn't have it. I watched as she cycled further away, until she had even passed the airport and was nearing the bend in the fjord. I think she was reminding me that this was her adventure as well, and not just mine.

Women are Vikings, too—you only have to think of Hallgerð and her famous refusal to give Gunnar a strand of her hair. The school's principal Ólína was similarly famous for her Nordic strength of character. Everyone knew her, and everyone had on hand a short biography of her life as well as an opinion about how well she suited the job of running a small school. She was very Icelandic, I was told. She would have things her way. She was not afraid of a fight. She didn't know when to stop.

Ingibjörg, the other English teacher, was noticeably more charismatic and loud—every morning, she walked into the teachers' common room singing Beatles songs. She had recently followed her husband Hermann, a local of the Westfjords, to Isafjörður. Her response to the quiet life in an isolated and closed town had been to emphasise her difference from the locals, which here meant being open and free with others. Hers was certainly not the Westfjords way, not the way of independent people; she had on only three occasions been invited into the locals' homes, once for each year she'd lived in the area.

It was a hard place for newcomers to fit in. But every Tuesday the teachers played volleyball, and for the whole time we lived in Isafjörður we made a point of joining in, however difficult the short walk to the sports centre became during the winter blizzards. After our very first game in late August, Olanda said, 'Ólína and Ingibjörg can't stand each other.' I asked how she could possibly know that—I hadn't detected any animosity. It was intuitive, she replied, but it was there. No woman would have doubted it.

At the time, I didn't think any more of it. But over time we returned to Olanda's first impression of Ólína and Ingibjörg again and again to explain and interpret a fight that would, during our year in the Westfjords, erupt in the school; it would distort not only our's, but the whole nation's, sense of Ísajörður. We were in for a difficult year.

Ingibjörg and Hermann were determined that we shouldn't feel isolated, and would invite us around to their place for coffee and dinner.

'You two must keep trying,' Ingibjörg said, although we hadn't said we weren't. 'This place may be different for you. Maybe you belong here. People realised very quickly that I don't.'

Towards the end of autumn, the couple asked us to join them in the annual sheep round-up. They had a share in an old farm building that they used only as a summerhouse, but they were bound by convention to help with the herding. It wouldn't be strenuous—Olanda and I wouldn't be doing much herding. All the same, arriving in jeans and joggers seemed to confirm a view among the others that we would be part of the herd, and more of a burden than the sheep. Ingibjörg led us to the farmhouse and found Wellingtons. Olanda's were quite luxurious, with woollen lining. Mine were two sizes too small, but better than joggers.

Apart from Ingibjörg, who giggled at our clothes and called us hopeless townies, there was a good deal of serious-ness in the air. Many of the herders were dressed in elaborate Lycra running outfits. Ingibjörg said we weren't to laugh at their tights as they would be taking to the upper reaches of the valley, as high even as the cliffs at the top of the surround-ing mountains. We, on the other hand, were to keep close to the river on the valley floor. It was very wet there, but com-pletely safe.

The method of shepherding used in such valley round-ups was wonderfully simple. There was no contact with the sheep. We just had to walk to the end of the valley and back again. That was it. The sheep would sense we were coming and stay a good distance ahead of us. If all went well they would stay in front of us right up to the farm gates. It was farming at a level that even we could manage. As the thin men in Lycra scrambled off into the gathering fog we too bounded away from our guardians. Olanda positively hopped.

'Don't go too quickly through this stuff,' I said.

'I'm fine.'

'Stick close. The mud can give way under foot.'

'Relax. I'm just here.' But in fact she was off, released into the countryside like a spring lamb. Except, one of her legs disappeared. The other was bent back on itself, looking for leverage.

'What did I say?'

'Help me,' she said. But she couldn't wait and swung the other leg around to give her some leverage on the mud. It sunk in, too.

'You haven't gone and stuck the other one in as well have you? You'll get pneumonia.'

'Get me out then!'

I began pulling her out.

'No, stop, stop!' she screamed. 'My boots are coming off.' I stopped for a moment. It was either her or the boots. 'Just pull,' she said.

Across the valley, on the other side of the river, one of the Lycra men was waving his walking stick. I gestured with a thumbs-up and called out, 'Yes, we're fine.'

No. He was urging us on. There was no mercy. We obeyed, Olanda barely able to walk in her sodden trousers. Half the lining of her boots, which I had recovered from the bog, still hung out.

'I hope he rips his tights,' said Olanda.

The encounter with the sheep was, as promised, late in coming and unglamorous. Two hours into our march we met an ancient, massively overweight sheep that had been left behind by the others. As I shooed it on, she growled and stomped.

'She doesn't growl at me,' said Olanda. 'It must be because you're a man.'

'What should I do?'

'Shoo louder,' she replied. I shooed louder.

Ingibjörg was watching from a ledge above. We should throw stones, she signalled.

'No,' I shouted back.

Ingibjörg's hand gestures became more deliberate, frustrated even. She began to throw stones towards us.

'You're kidding me,' I said. 'I'm not throwing stones at an old sheep.' Ingibjörg made her way towards us through the scree.

'I don't think you're ever going to be farmers,' she said as she reached us. 'Not at the sheep. Just around her. To make a noise.' We celebrated when the stones didn't work for her, either. And then we waited until the farmer came. He picked up the sheep in his arms and carried it over to a red van that was parked by a fence.

'We've got her into trouble, haven't we?' asked Olanda.

'We don't know what he's going to do with her. I'm sure she isn't the only difficult sheep in the herd,' I said.

'None of them want to go back in after summer,' said Ingibjörg, 'especially not the older ones.'

Olanda was given a change of clothes, and we walked together to the newest of the farmhouses, where a late lunch was put on for all the herders. Laid out on a crisscross of tables were a dozen legs of lamb, served with strawberry jam, peas and boiled potatoes.

'Isn't it good to be back in Iceland?' asked the farmer's wife. Yes, it was. The reasons were not always easy to explain, but I thought there were only a few who wouldn't have enjoyed being half-Icelandic on that autumn day in the Westfjords.

As we left the farm the fog cleared, revealing the pale, damp colours of the season. Low clouds remained and crowned the valley in blushes of orange and auburn. On the cliff tops, a single Lycra man remained, fetching in the rogue sheep, which from the valley floor were barely the size of toy figures.

There was a famous line in the *The Saga of Gísli*, a work local to the area, about all the streams running down to the fjord, and I now understood why it seemed such a natural metaphor. The streams in the saga stood for fate, for the point at which your course in life seemed inevitable, but also for what the mountains did to everyone all the time: shaping their relation to the sea and the narrow stretches of farmable land that met it. In the Westfjords, you were forever being tipped into the water. But the fjords also sharpened your perception of the sky, which was shaped by the flat, sharp ledges of the mountains.

In September the northern lights began to show. Early one evening as we walked home from volleyball we noticed the fine streaks of green light gathering over the fjord. The light intensified and moved very quickly towards where we were standing, until just a few minutes later the pulses had collected above us. They reared ferociously across low clouds that had settled in the fjord and then, as if a match had been put to it, red flames engulfed the clouds. We stood at the door of our apartment shaking with cold.

'I just can't believe it,' said Olanda. 'I can't believe anything could be so beautiful.' I looked across to see her crying with excitement.

The heaths and the mountains closed you off from the rest of the world, but they also gathered you in the increased activity of the town, as had the fierceness of the northern lights. My students, I noticed, would scoot off during breaks between classes, snatching an hour here and there to fulfil myriad other obligations. It hadn't occurred to me that life in a small town would be more hectic than life in the city.

'But we have the time to be busy,' one said to me.

To my surprise I was becoming more and more involved in the pleasing busyness of rural life. Ingibjörg, I felt, was a little wrong about the place. I found myself robbed of my long-held preference for solitary pursuits by joining all of the group activities I could—volleyball, indoor soccer, walking groups, kayaking, and even the local music scene—half of which seemed to be organised by one of my students, Halldór. He and I did some gigs together at the town's one and only café bar, Langi Mangi, and the miracle of my existence, as already reported in the local and national media, was confirmed again: a man who sings has moved to Ísafjörður, went the reports.

◄━━━

There was a lot of heavy drinking. Both the teachers and the students had a reputation for unruly behaviour on social nights. I found this a rather quaint idea, mainly because the students in Iceland struck me as too kind for wildness, until Ólína suspended seventy of them for drunkenness during the annual school camp. Apparently, their behaviour had been so crazed that the camp supervisor, fearing what the students would do to him if they had their way, locked himself in a cabin and wouldn't come out until late the next morning.

The reaction of the townsfolk seemed on the side of the students. What did Ólína expect young people to do? What did she think students at the other schools did? It was a nonargument, but I wondered too whether we teachers were any better. Our social evenings all began with the same respectable dinner of lamb, potatoes and beans, and perhaps a little wine. It was the penance for what was to come: a descent into drunkenness and Icelandic pop songs as steady and unforgiving as the fall of the mountains. By midnight, we were singing our way through the unsteady streets of Ísafjörður to Langi Mangi café and still more Bubbi Morthens covers.

The students came back from their suspensions, not chastened but not embittered by the experience, either. They seemed to accept that this was how the school would be under

Ólína, and that the old days of rural leniency were over. It's just that they weren't yet ready to change how they behaved. That there was more fighting to come was inevitable, and yet few of us, guessed that it would be a fight between the teachers that would define this year in the school's life.

By October, the nights were becoming long but the fjord was at its most intensely clear. It became a landscape of sharp contrasts: the water, the brown cliffs, the snow, and the sky, as always pinched by a narrowing fjord. Excited by the arrival of snow, Olanda and I rode with hangovers along an old road, following it in the direction of where most of the snow had seemed to fall. Chasing one false summit after another, we finally gave up and settled on some flat, sheltered ground, and lay in the sun with a wide view of the fjord beneath us.

'How long do you think you could live here?' I asked.

'We both wanted to come,' replied Olanda. 'I just need to get some work. I'll go mad sitting at home all day.'

'What would you be prepared to do?'

'Just about anything now. I'll ask at the fish factories.'

'Please don't do that.'

'Why not? I could do it until the summer and then stop in time for the tourist season.'

'But not the fish factory. What will I tell your parents, that I brought you all this way just so that you could gut fish?'

The school's commemoration of the old, harsh life of fishing was the annual boat race between teachers and students, held each year on *Sjómannadagur*, or 'Seaman's Day'. The long rowing boats had once been used on the open waters of the North Atlantic, and they would race from the spit to an imagined finishing line near the school buildings.

A men's and women's team was organised; during evening practices in the lead-up to the big day, we called out across the water to each other. My male colleagues were full of rosy-cheeked confidence, but our gibes at the women's team seemed defensive to me. Their boat looked much better in the water than ours. It was being run by Ólína, after all, whose stroke-counting cut through the evening air with a determination that our helmsman Jóhann noted with awe. She was every bit the magistrate's daughter.

Siggi, Ólína's husband, was the most experienced of our crew, and he assured us that the women had the better, lighter boat. And of course were lighter in it, too. In any case, he continued, where were the students? They were going to be our competition on the day, and they weren't even practicing yet. It may have been years since the teachers had won, but the students' complacency gave us a chance.

I wasn't so sure. Jóhann's stroke-counting only ever satisfied one person at a time, and our boat was so end-heavy that Siggi in the bow was raised a foot clear of the water. We spent much too long debating technique. The debate, rather than airing important issues, suggested that we didn't actually have a technique. The question, 'How do we start the race without stopping or going around in circles?' marked a low point.

'You stick the oar into the water as deep as possible and then take a great, long stroke,' said Stefan, the German teacher.

'No,' I said. 'Take short, sharp strokes and gradually extend to longer ones.'

'No, no,' said the others. 'No more from the Australian, please.'

By race day, we were beginning to show the results of all of our training: we were rubbish. But perhaps this was the year, after all. The students still hadn't trained, not even once. We cruised through the early rounds, and in the final, lined up against seven eighteen-year-olds, whose combined body weight was about the same as mine.

'We need consistent rowing. Don't worry too much about power. Technique is everything,' Siggi said.

'Well, we'll never beat these guys on fitness,' said Rúnar.

'They are fit but they haven't practised,' added Jóhann. Siggi looked from Jóhann to the rest of the group.

'Whatever you do, you must keep to the tempo that Jóhann sets. And Jóhann, you mustn't count too fast. Don't get excited. Keep it slow and steady, and we might manage this.'

We were off. Almost fantastically, we got a clean start. Jóhann led on with measured, audible counting. The students were winded, and lagged. I looked across and even noticed a touch of panic. They thought we were going to be tired, old men. The day was ours. But then, as perhaps was always going to be the case, disaster struck.

Excited by the possibility of victory, Jóhann raised the tempo. We began to flap. We were thrown out of rhythm, stuck still on top of the sea, plunging hopelessly deep. Behind me,

Rúnar's handle dug into the small of my back, and my cry of pain released an explosion of abuse from the others.

'What the hell are you doing, Jóhann!?'

'Gradual build-up, gradual build-up,' came the call from a desperate cox.

'They haven't practised,' cried Siggi.

'Yes, they have. You can see it,' replied Stefan. 'They have.'

'It's okay,' called Jóhann. 'We can still do this.'

No, we couldn't. The students, sensing our distress, put in a late push for the line. And won.

Sjómannadagur was the first of many such rituals that we joined. Icelanders are rather taken with formal expressions of shared nostalgia for the old days, and as the returning native it was expected that I participate. It was the formal part of my education and initiation. In an Icelandic academic year I was to undergo the privations of centuries, from the sheep herding and rowing to the vile delicacies of the winter festival.

It was also clear to me that they were showing off; that part of the appeal of having me there was the presence of foreign eyes. It had been the same when Gísli took me to the president's lodge at Bessastaðir, and showed off his farm-life childhood. At the same time as I was being introduced to my heritage, I was reminded of its distance, and of a question common to all returning migrants: at what point were you too far out of the culture to make a meaningful return?

18

DIGGING

One of the other teachers said the soft light of winter suited her. She lived in Flateyri, the nearby village of Bergur's ancestry, and each day she commuted through a long tunnel that had been cut through the mountains to Isafjörður. Flateyri sat on the edge of a wider fjord than ours, and even in mid-winter it still had direct sunlight on the clear days. I envied her, as I did those with cars who could at least drive to the top of the mountains for a peek at the sun. Now that it was November, the sun was completely invisible from us and wouldn't, it was said, return until February.

Sharp frosts and snow storms arrived, coinciding with the Christmas holidays and an exodus of the professionals in town, many of them geologists and ichthyologists. The inbound flights were busy, too, with locals returning from their jobs in Reykjavík. The weather worsened yet more, then came flight cancellations. People had to brace themselves for long, dangerous drives across the heaths to the south. Rán, an Icelandic teacher, who didn't at all like the soft light of winter and had booked a holiday in Spain in order to escape it, looked out over the fjord with a scowl.

'It's only the thought of sunshine that's getting me through the semester,' she said. 'Even if I have to drive for two days, I'm going to make that flight.'

Ingibjörg was less determined but just as excited about her trip, which this year would take her to France, a spiritual home for her. She'd been asked to chaperone a niece to a music school there. It would mean getting through her exam papers quickly, generally a good thing for teachers, who otherwise dragged out their marking. She too watched the weather more carefully than usual. Olanda and I shared a little in their fate, as we had organised to spend Christmas with Bergur and Rut in Reykjavík. During a break in the storms, we and half a dozen other teachers had calls from the airport to get to the plane for a quick escape from the fjord.

Beneath us the countryside of the western coastline was brown and frozen, the dams and lakes shattered by lines of cracked ice. It was a life even more isolated than ours, on farms on the low-lying islands of Breiðafjörður and on the thin, rocky peninsulas that lined Snæfellsnes. In summer, I knew, they would have glorious days of seclusion and separateness. But what did you tell yourself in winter?

Reykjavík was as cold as Ísafjörður, but it hadn't snowed, and the days seemed much longer now that we saw the sun again. A protracted sunrise began at ten and ended, just after lunch, with the start of an equally long sunset. The pond downtown was frozen solid, and the surface had been smoothed out for skaters—towards dark, families came down and put on their skates, using their car headlights as torches. Orange spotlights lit a skating arena about the size of a football field, but kids, animals, and calm parents were spread across the entire pond. Clusters formed here and there, a scene atypically open and relaxed, Australian even. People mingled.

Laugavegur was carnivalesque too. With darkness coming on so early, the small shops and cafés of the main street, which sometimes looked a little tired, took on the cosy, even glamorous appearance of a side street in Copenhagen. It was a pleasant deception, especially after the remoteness of Ísafjörður. We walked from shop to shop, stopping here and there for drinks. Lights from above blurred in the cold night air, as though they'd been photographed by a shaking hand. The Christmas decorations had their desired effect, drawing in a constant stream of happy-looking people who walked or drove slowly through the night.

The festivities peaked on the night of Thorláksmessa, 'The Day of St Thorlák', the patron saint of Iceland. It fell on the 23rd of December, the anniversary of his death. The Icelandic reserve and seriousness seemed less present tonight than on any other—it didn't take an expert eye to see that everyone was out flirting, gossiping, and exchanging information that did more for their personal honour than the general good of the community, or its religious virtue. It was, in a way, summer at Thingvellir, and the year Gunnar and Hallgerð met and sat down to talk about Gunnar's trip to Norway, and about the fine things he'd brought back to Iceland. It was the hundred conversations that had surrounded me and my mother, and the mystery of my father.

As always, Kári suggested a drive to Thingvellir—there had been heavy snowfalls and he wanted to see it while the snow was still fresh and yet to be trodden. The nearby ski runs were open; the snow buggies were out. As we passed the outskirts of town and began the climb into Mossfellsheiði, we joined a line of big men in big coats and big cars. Through their tail-gates shone the reflections of shovels and heavy-weather gear, and Kári said that for many of them the idea was to get stuck on purpose so that they could test out their equipment. I joked that this sounded a lot like me, and that I was always looking for ways of getting stuck in Iceland.

We had left Reykjavík in the dark, but gradually as we approached the park the in-between light of the northern winter broke in among the white mountains. We entered a landscape of rifts, coated to the edges in the pure snow of morning, with the sky and the ground joined by rice-paper light. It was Iceland, but it was also a place that lay beyond it, in a locked-away landscape that offered your own disappearance into the indecisive play of the light. You came here to think about fewer things, but also to think about them more clearly.

While we were in Reykjavík, our friends in Ísafjörður had to bunker down—reports were coming in of the heaviest snow-falls in ten years. The last time it had snowed as much, in 1995, avalanches had devastated the villages of Súðavik and Flateyri; thirty-four people had died. Since then barriers had been built around the most dangerous areas—our afternoon rides in the autumn had taken us along an earth wall that had been erected around Tungudalur. But nervousness remained. The most precarious combination, soft snow on top of ice, was again in place. The papers said it would only be a matter of time before people were evacuated.

It was a relief to be away from the worst of the storms, but it was also somehow wrong to be safe and comfortable at Bergur and Rut's. We'd only lived in the Westfjords for a few months, but not being there during the storms felt traitor-ous. The northerlies that were causing so much trouble in the Westfjords brought only clear days to Reykjavík.

While we waited for flights to resume, Bergur filled me in on the various weather catastrophes that had visited his life of touring Iceland. Between his tales of sliding off the roads, most of which were only funny, came a more dispiriting refrain about the recent lack of real winters. In the context of year after year of mild, wet weather, the severity of this Christmas was welcomed. Bergur, I knew, lived as much in his recollections of past adven-tures as he did in his present life, a tamed routine of visiting the office in the mornings, coming home for lunch, and making a slow return to work in the afternoons. Beneath his nostalgia was an urgent need to reconnect with something in his past.

Perhaps that was the reason we were such good friends, and why I had come to love him and his family so deeply. His conjuring of the past was as central for him as it was for me. A dozen or so narratives circled him constantly. He often spoke about his mother and father and their move from Flateyri to Reykjavík. This connection with the Westfjords seemed crucial: it made him more than a mere Reykjavíkingur. A plaque, *Bergshús*, or 'Bergur's House', had been placed on one of the older line of sea-facing houses in the village. It was a source of great pride—his father's old house was being commemorated through the son, and more than once he asked whether I'd been to see it. I would reply that I had, and the story and his father's departure from Flateyri would begin again.

Such were the divides in his life. The Westfjords, it seemed, remained in the corner of his mind. It was a home of sorts. Flateyri was to him what Reykjavík was to me: a place to be in love with, an origin myth. But what did that mean?

Partly it meant this question, 'Will you stay in Iceland?', which I was being asked nearly every day, by Bergur and Rut, their children, my sisters, colleagues, and strangers at the swimming pools. The question I asked myself, though, had changed, and I was becoming less concerned about what I would do. The task was to understand how this feeling for Iceland was to exist within me—not, so much, how I was to exist in Iceland. Was there a difference between feeling at home and being home?

Love was a vague term, I knew. But many people, I gathered, were used to feeling at home in the country of their birth, but not always being in love with it. I seemed to have it the other way around: I was forever falling more deeply in love with Iceland, at the same time as I seemed as far away from knowing how to stay.

The truth was, I missed something about Brisbane that in

fifteen years of living there I hadn't ever properly registered. I missed its openness. When people sat outside to eat and drink, they didn't always talk about very much in particular—to do so wasn't quite the Brisbane way. But they talked about their nothings in a generous way, and presented them with such a self-effacing irony that in the course of a night you came nearer to serious topics. In Brisbane, the canopies were tall and evergreen, and I hadn't before realised what that must mean about the undergrowth that sustained them.

In the mornings we checked for updates, but the flights to Ísafjörður were always cancelled. One morning, after Rut read out the weather report from *Morgunblaðið*, she turned to the astrology section.

'Look at yours, Olanda,' she called out. 'It says a business opportunity is coming up.' Sure enough, a little later that morning the phone rang. It was the Ísafjörður Sushi Factory, calling to ask if she'd like a job.

'You will be making sushi to be snap-frozen and exported to our foreign customers,' the manager told her. It wasn't exactly a business opportunity, but they made a point of explaining that this would be a step up from regular fish factory work.

'There is no fish-gutting experience needed for this job.'

I asked her not to take it. It would be horrible. She took it.

'I'm not spending the rest of the winter indoors,' she told me.

After a week of cancellations, came a break in the weather, a window of an hour or so between the storm finishing up in the north and starting up in the south. We needed to get to the airport quickly—three planes would leave together in the space of half an hour. Rut rushed us to a terminal building straining with Westfjorders, including half-a-dozen teachers bronzed with Canary Island tans.

The pilot was unnaturally cheery, and this worried me. He conceded that it would be a bumpy flight with a rough descent, especially when we turned into the Djúp, the long fjord that ran the length of the smaller ones. This is where we'd start to feel the wind. Getting the plane down would, he said, depend on the last couple of minutes, especially as we took on the less predictable winds that came off the mountains of our fjord. We weren't to be worried by the plane's heaving motion. Any sign of a major problem and we'd return to Reykjavík.

'What's a major problem going to be?' asked Olanda.

'I suppose he means a crash,' I replied. 'That would be a major problem.'

The turbulence was actually terrible the whole way, but as we got down into the Djúp and towards the mountains it was simply extraordinary. We were rattling, and bouncing violently, as though in the grip of the trolls that had once made the hollows in the fjords. We heard the strain of full throttle, and we pulled out of the fjord, heaving back over the mountains. Around us there was lots of crying and vomiting, and a bitter, 'God help us,' from a colleague.

'What's happening?' asked Olanda.

'We're going around, I think.'

She reached for her vomit bag with one hand and my arm with the other.

'No, it's okay, I think we're going back,' I said. The aircraft banked, and was hit by a hard gust. There was a loud bang, a car crash sound, and we lurched to the left.

'Well,' said the pilot. 'Sorry about that. We'll have another go, and if it's as bad again, we'll return to Reykjavík. The plane ahead of us seems to have made it down okay.' I reminded myself that pilots were wealthy, happy people—they had families, no reason to die.

Again we bounced down into the fjord. Olanda was crying, the woman in the seat behind us had begun to wail. But we landed, and the plane itself seemed to breathe a sigh of relief as it did so. There was no round of applause. To clap wouldn't have been right. We wanted to evacuate.

Our street, when we got to it, was still open but barely reachable. The taxi driver wouldn't stop the car for fear of being stuck, and so he asked us to get out while the car continued to creep along. Our front door was buried under seven feet of snow. Alma, our landlady, handed me a shovel and said it was time to *moka*, 'to clear the snow'. I called Rúnar for help and for an hour we dug our way inside. The next morning, I spent two more hours digging a second path to one of our windows so we could get some light into the apartment.

Only the main road into town was kept clear, and for over

a week no-one in Ísafjörður could drive—in fact, most of the cars in town were buried. No matter what time of the day you went out, you found your neighbours hobbling along the firming snow, or clutching onto walls, pushing through mounds of drift snow. The town graveyard, which had at first been buried up to its walls, finally began to re-emerge with its Christmas lights more or less intact, presenting a puzzle of reflected headstones across the packed snow in the evenings.

As the snow melted, streams formed across the ice that had lay beneath it, and it became almost impossible to stay on our feet. One morning on the way to school I turned out of our street and down a short hill, and lost my footing. It began as a slow slide along the gutter—I was in a little river of my own, and it carried me calmly away from the corner I had just passed. I hooked out an arm, but this did no good. The pavement was close, but each time I reached for it I moved further towards the middle of the road. Eventually I joined a main current that ran down the centre of the street. It was hopeless.

With some horror I felt the headlights of a car settle on my back. I spread myself out, and tried to get my legs to cycle me to the side. But I simply couldn't get my arms high enough into the air to signal for the car to stop. I was in for a slow death.

But no. A door opened at my side.

'Pull yourself in,' said a woman's voice. I grasped the step up to the passenger door and dragged myself towards the warmth of the cabin.

'Going up or down?' she asked.

The storm had been terrible, but a repeat of the disaster of 1995 was averted. An avalanche in the nearby village of Hnífsdalur destroyed a number of farm buildings, but the owners had escaped in time. In fact, the most disturbing news of the winter break emerged from the school. Ólína had issued Ingibjörg an official warning over her marking of the December exam papers—apparently there were errors, and overall the marks were much too high. In reply, Ingibjörg went to the Teachers' Union who, it was whispered, was fed up with Ólína. They stated their full support for Ingibjörg, and the fight that Olanda had felt coming during our first volleyball game began in earnest.

The two husbands, I now learnt, were cousins; so this was in part a family dispute. People said that when Hermann and Ingibjörg had first come to live in the town, there had been a great show of warmth between the couples, and that they'd socialised regularly. There had followed a bad falling out; no-one was quite sure what it was over. Another rumour said that it was only now, when I was at hand as an alternative head of English, that the dispute had moved into the workplace.

It had all the makings of a saga feud: family conflict, a clash of outlooks, a minor triggering incident, and preparedness on the part of the protagonists to destroy everyone around them. In the months that followed, that was how it played out. In the place of the sagas' verbal duelling and poetic insults came tit-for-tat appeals to the national press, which consumed the fight with glee and published weekly, sometimes daily updates on the life of the school, including loud and ugly rows in the coffee room and at every staff meeting from February to May.

The staff split into two camps, those for epic and those for romance, and the school went toxic.

The daily grind of gossip and paranoia made work life outside the classroom unbearable. No-one could think of anything but the dispute, and every comment was interpreted in its light. I couldn't quite shake the thought that the whole thing was provincial in a way that Iceland had turned into an art form: the leads had long-standing enmities that were almost impossible to understand, while the side-players were often as implicated in the history of past grudges as the main adversaries. As such, I didn't think there was any point in taking sides and, if I thought it could have helped, I would have thrown my saga editions at them all. I liked just about everyone at the school, and despised the way they were fighting.

So instead of fighting, I joined Olanda each day on her morning walks to work, and to some extent these moments of quiet along the fjord redeemed the early months of 2005 from the turmoil at work. We left home at six-thirty and followed the smell of gutted fish along the northern side of the spit to the harbour area. Few others walked to work, but we were never entirely on our own. Even in the worst weather, some rode their bikes and fell over in slow motion whenever they hit snow.

We gained half an hour's light each week and so our morning walks became brighter. By March, they were in full daylight again and the town celebrated with its Sun Coffee Festival. It was like rejoining the world.

Olanda loved her job at the sushi factory. The tasks were menial, and she came home with a backache, but the others who worked there were, she said, beautiful—mainly immigrants from Thailand, Poland and Germany. They laughed through the whole shift, while my colleagues, who spent their days embroiled in the conflict at the school, found it hard to believe that the migrant community was as open as Olanda said.

'I don't know how you can be friends with the migrants,' said one teacher. 'They only come here for the work, they send their money home, and keep to themselves the whole time they're here. They don't bother learning the language.' The students, I found, were just as resolute in their prejudice.

I could have replied that she got along with them because she was a migrant herself, but I suppose that would have been a disingenuous line. We had it much easier than the other new arrivals. Instead I replied that this was a classic case of the locals not seeing what was obvious to every traveller: Iceland was a small, closed society.

One of the teachers, Valdimar, was keen to improve relations between the migrants and locals, and he ran the local migrant group. He asked me to play some songs for the group's social meetings—anything, he said, to get the numbers up. I went along and sang, with no effect on the numbers. Those who came obviously wanted to be pleased and they smiled and made jokes. But as the meeting was conducted entirely in Icelandic and English, both incomprehensible to most of them, over the course of the morning the expressions on the participants' faces turned from goodwill to vacant irritation.

I see now I was experiencing something that I hadn't really

prepared for. Iceland was in many respects a country just like all others. It cherished its borders, and its right to protect them. Many people didn't want anything to change, and clung to an Iceland that did more to exclude than include.

19

Kolbrún, Bergur's older daughter, picked us up from the airport and drove us out to the hospital in Keflavík.

'We're not sure how much longer she's got,' she said as we
followed the airport road. 'It could be days or hours. But not
weeks any more.'

'Is she distressed?' I asked.

'She's had a lot of visitors. And she's had the chance to say
goodbye to just about everyone she wants to.'

'That's good. I have a letter from Mum.'

The first thing Patricia said to me when we arrived at the
hospital was that she was the first person Mum had told about
her pregnancy.

'We'd only met a short while before,' she added. 'I think
your mother confided in me almost as a stranger would.'

'I admit I have sometimes wondered why she was so open
with you,' I replied. 'The two of you are so different.'

'It was Iceland,' said Patricia. 'We were both hopeless about
Iceland.'

Theirs had been a bumpy friendship. When my mother had come to Iceland for her sixtieth birthday, they'd fallen out again, another of the long line of fallings-out among the army of secretaries. This time it had been over a trivial matter. My mother hadn't wanted to spend the night at Patricia's, and this had offended Patricia, who attributed some hostility to the refusal. My mother, like many of Patricia's friends, was afraid to tell her the truth, which was that she couldn't bear the thought of a night with all of Patricia's pets. But they'd been friends for too long for one of them to die with this rift left unhealed, and that's why I was here, in part, as Mum's emissary.

It was 2005, but I still saw Patricia through the rather glamorous frame of the 1970s ex-pat girls in Iceland. Marriage had pinned most of them down here but Patricia, like my mother, had loved the place, and felt at home here and only here. There had been no crisis to drive her either to Iceland or away again, no wanderer's curse—she was simply one of those who saw Iceland as inevitable.

I handed her Mum's letter. It was a short note saying that Mum hoped the two of them could be friends again. Patricia took it well and folded the letter into a book to read again later. I felt a desperate need to press pause. Soon the note would cease to be alive between her and my mother; it would become part of the other belongings she left behind—an odd bookmark in the last thing she read.

But I wasn't after the past anymore, I saw that. I didn't want to rewind, or recreate the world as it had existed during my childhood. What I wanted was a childhood sensation. The one where your surroundings—your Iceland—are simply an implicit part of action, unreflective and living inside you rather than around you. The one where you aren't making sense of Iceland, because Iceland is woven in. Patricia still had that. She said she was happy that she would die in the place where the sensation had always existed.

Back home, Rúnar called me the next day to say he'd bought himself a new kayak, which he claimed was better than the old one because it was easier to turn over in the water. The purchase meant that he could lend me his old one, which he said was good, because it was less likely to roll. I was told to dress warmly and meet at the canoe shed at the end of the spit at seven-thirty on Sunday.

At eight, while the town was still coiled in a deep sleep, Rúnar and his father pushed me out into the fjord. After Rúnar had made a few of the rolls he so liked he joined me in the deep. We slipped through still water, paddling inland towards Tungudalur. Ours was the only human noise in the fjord.

The water was dark brown and silky, but it flickered with the bird life of the fjord. Deflections of white wings crossed our bows. Out in the middle, I again got a glimpse of the fisherman's view of the town and the mountains that I'd had during our practices for the rowing race. It was the default perspective of a thousand years of settlement, and it made the mountains less intimidating, the sound more welcoming—a retreat from the open waters beyond. The fjord became a circumference, a shelter, and not a place of avalanches and storms.

When I got back in, I wrote an email to Patricia telling her that we'd seen early arriving puffins flying low across the water. She replied an hour later that she could picture them, and that she'd begun to feel much better. Who knew, perhaps there would be some time yet. The next email came from Kolbrún, on the following day, to say that Patricia had died.

Again I flew south, this time for the funeral. Kolbrún helped with the service, Kári was one of the coffin bearers, and I joined Bergur, Rut and Rakel in the front row; in the end it seemed that we were as close as Patricia had come to having an Icelandic family. Judith brought Gestur, who as far as I knew still had the largest collection of Elvis records in Iceland. Molly and Nanci were too sick to come. The rest of the congregation were locals from Vogar, Patricia's village for thirty years, or workers from the American Base, once Patricia's employer, the source of beer, cheap cigarettes and the other minor luxuries from the Cod War period, before the northern Puritanism had eased a little.

The army of secretaries was, I felt, much diminished by Patricia's passing and by the illness of the others. Theirs had once been a perfect universe, like a good book; they suited each other so well, especially in the isolation of the new Iceland. And for a while I had been one of their projects— my isolation had matched theirs, and they had become more than my friends.

The coffin was placed in the ground and a line of mourners formed to stand above it to make the sign of the cross. It didn't seem quite right for Patricia, even if she was religious. It was all too serious, sombre, and Scandinavian. The army's faith had always been in laughter, gossip and disgruntlement, and in the bond of the outsiders who knew they could never leave.

My flight back to Ísafjörður was crowded with musicians. It was time for the town's annual rock festival, *Aldrei fór ég suður*, or 'I never went south'. The title came from a song by Bubbi Morthens—Iceland's working hero musician—about a man who stays in his village too long. He can't move, or escape the fixed patterns of fishing, salting and bunking down for the dark winters. Year after year he is left to make the most of the bleakness.

I was not so defiant, I was not an extremist, and I didn't believe in the death or honour creed of those around me who were holding on in the Westfjords. I would bend to the situation on the ground, and the Viking warriors Ólína and Ingibjörg could have it, and fight until they buried themselves. Olanda and I were heading south the minute we could.

Suddenly, the dead grass of winter was being pushed out of the way by new shoots, almost mint green at their base. The sound of heavy water falling down from the heaths returned, and the noise of people touching up their summerhouses echoed through the fjord. Bumblebees arrived and patrolled the daffodils and tulips. The whole of May was cloudless.

My last-year students, dressed in farewell sumo-wrestler outfits, finished a rowdy morning call at our place and headed off to wake up the next victims. It was the annual ritual of waking up the teachers on the students' last day. Many were wearing mittens, and some liberties in the costume had been taken in other areas—the coolest wouldn't be seen without retro police sunglasses. Halldór, now my friend and very much the musician in the group, led them down the hill in front of our place as they took what were really their first steps to Reykjavík, and mine.

'Oh Dr Kári, oh Dr Kári,' they sang as a goodbye. All that was left to do was to climb the troll's seat, the hollow in the mountain that I'd been looking at from my office since the day we arrived.

Olanda and I rode our bikes around the fjord and past the airport, and rested them against a sign that pointed to a thin track that followed one of the growing hillside streams. It was only half an hour to the base of the hollow, and we stopped by a residue of snow and set up a picnic.

It wasn't really warm enough—about six degrees Celsius—but the sun was out and we found shelter from the wind in the walls of the great hollow around us. Below us in the valley lay the runway and the end of the spit. Above us a steep slope of scree and boulders. Now and then, we heard the scattering of stones as they tumbled down the face of the scree.

We were getting away before the town had a chance to recover from the fight at the school. Rúnar for one said he could never leave as things stood, but I had accepted a teaching job in the capital. Our last look at the fjord would have to stand in place of a better goodbye to Ísafjörður and my students. They still had another full year of the feud ahead of them, one that would see both sides claim vindication, and both Ólína and Ingibjörg resign their positions at the school. The next day, we boarded the Fokker 50 to Reykjavík.

20

FATHERHOOD

Despite some of the difficulties that have come with it, I am a little proud of being the result of a love affair. My parents chose to have it in secret in order to keep it alive; discovery would almost certainly have ended it. My mother protected Gísli, I think in part because that protected them. Their affair changed their sense of who they were, because it changed their conception of how they loved. The basement apartment in Sólvallagata—'Sun Fields Street'—was the place of a journey—into another version of themselves, and into another possibility in life. Even now, it's a side of my parents that I only barely understand, and perhaps that's the way it should be.

Becoming known as Gísli's son has allowed me to relax in the business of knowing. By late 2005, when Olanda and I had been living again in Reykjavík for some months, another event came to take the emphasis off revealing the past and onto discovering what lay ahead. She had a fair idea that she was 'un-light', or *ólétt* as the Icelandic phrased it.

The all-night chemist wasn't far. We pushed our way through the tunnel of wind that ran down the front of the block, and returned with a pregnancy test kit and its instructions. The colour on the test was indecisive.

'Does this mean you're pregnant?' I asked.

'I think it means it doesn't know.'

The next day as I went to work, Olanda took the bus to Seltjarnarnes. In one of those little coincidences that seem to mean something, the only clinic that could fit her in was by the site of my family's ancestral farm. Perhaps like my ancestors had once done, she had to pull herself along a fence to get through the snowstorm and into the doctors' surgery.

'Yes, you're pregnant,' said the doctor. 'You're going to have a baby in Iceland.' She said she didn't need to do a test. 'I can give you one if you like. But if you think you're pregnant, then I'd say you are pregnant.'

It was a busy winter. There was plenty of overtime going at work, and I now also taught part-time at the University of Iceland. Most nights I worked until ten. Olanda also did late shifts at her new job at the swimming pool Laugardalur. Often I'd meet her just before she clocked off and have a night-time swim while she was packing up. It was perfect; I had the pool to myself and the cold air on my shoulders. The hazy pool lights at the bottom inverted the world, with the darkness above a floor of steam and moonlight.

In the spring, we began our prenatal classes. They were

run in English for couples like us; mainly, it was the wives who were foreign, captured and brought to Iceland by husbands who unlike me seemed quite sure there wasn't anything wrong with living here. The instructor was large and very fine, but merciless in her convictions about male stupidity. We were told again and again that there was nothing that our wives could ask that was too much.

'If she tells you to leave, you leave. If she tells you to come back, come back. If she says, "shut the fuck up," then what do you do?'

'Shut the fuck up,' we repeated from our beanbags.

'Good. You're learning. And when you think she might be complaining too much, just imagine a bowling ball being shoved up your anus.'

It was uncompromising instruction. If I couldn't imagine the bowling ball, I could believe that it was going to be hard to have a first child so far away from your parents and siblings. And occasionally it showed. The distance from Reykjavík to Brisbane appeared in a faraway look that would, if only for a moment, defeat Olanda's excitement about becoming a mother.

He would be born in July, in high summer. Whether because of the endless light of June, or worrying about how Olanda was coping with being so far from home, I slept little, and long after she'd gone to bed I was still tracing the bike paths that followed the Reykjavík shoreline out to Seltjarnarnes.

June was cold, and the days seldom got into double digits. At midnight, the sun hung just above the horizon and lit the seaweed and the dune grass along the northern beach-heads. Behind me, the Reykjanes peninsula and the dormant volcanoes that extended to Keflavík turned purple. The golfers were out. Kayaks, and even the odd swimmer, paddled between the eider ducks, which at last redeemed their icy winters with a frenzy of diving for a sudden abundance of food beneath.

'Kári,' Olanda called out, 'I think he's coming.' I checked the small clock at the side of my bed. It was three thirty-eight am. She was breathing herself through a long contraction.

'Oh, good. You remembered to breathe.'

'Yes, I remembered.' The prenatal classes had emphasised this, repeatedly. Breathe, breathe, breathe. During the contraction. During the labour. During the birth. It was, apparently, the best thing you could do. It relaxed you, calmed you, and helped the body do its work. Its work! She had insisted that the body knew its work. If only you remembered to breathe.

'Should I call the hospital?' I asked.

'No, not yet. We have to wait until the contractions are closer together.'

'Do you want something? A cup of tea? Some food?'

'Not food. Tea would be good.' She was up out of bed, sitting near a mountain of pillows that for the past weeks had been placed around every curve of her body.

'Are you sure I can't get you something to eat?'

'No. No. I can't seem to forget what the instructor said.'

'You mean about the pooing?'

'Yes, the pooing. I don't want his first moment in this world to be all about poo.'

The instructor had told us that most of the women in the room would poo during birth, as the pressure on the anus was so great. The room looked away.

'I know it might not sound very nice,' the instructor went on, 'but, really, it's a natural part of the process. Your body knows its work. You mustn't think you've done anything wrong if baby comes out with poo around.'

Olanda wasn't so sure. She was determined to go to the toilet before we left for the hospital. Clear the bowels before the big moment.

'Okay. But you won't leave it too late, will you?' I said. She didn't answer; another contraction was coming on. She held out her tea cup for me to hold. I put it down on the floor, and then jotted down the time of the contraction in a notebook that I had kept open, especially for this moment. Twelve minutes had passed since the last one. Less intense, too.

It had only just passed four in the morning. There had been rain during the night, but the clouds were breaking up, and some sunshine was reflected in the dark, wet tar of the street outside. There wasn't much traffic but because of the endless light of the July days, the morning strollers were out already. It was a good time to walk.

At six, the contractions began to intensify and lengthen. One-minute-long contractions were, apparently, the ones to watch for. That's when you rang the hospital.

'Maternity ward,' said the midwife on the other end of the phone.

'My wife's contractions have begun,' I explained. 'They're not regular, yet—sometimes every seven or eight minutes, sometimes every ten or twelve. But she's in a lot of pain, and the contractions are getting longer. Up to a minute long, now.'

'We're at the end of a shift here. It would be better if she waited until the next shift came on.'

'I see. When would that be, then?'

'Call again at eight.' I looked around for Olanda.

'Where have you gone?' I asked.

'I'm on the toilet.' Then, she screamed.

'They said to wait until the shift change.'

'You're kidding me.' She looked up from the toilet. Her arm was extended hard against the basin. 'Please, call back.'

Everything was in place: hospital, notebook, taxi. I was dressed, Olanda was dressed, and her overnight bag was by the door. The only thing left was to get her off the toilet. She sat there in a crash-landing position. The screams were guttural.

'Darling, the taxi's coming. It'll be here in five minutes.'

'Good. Good.'

'That means you have to get off the toilet.'

'I know.' She wasn't moving.

'Please get off the toilet.'

'No.' I waited. Another contraction. I heard the taxi arrive. Olanda was getting up.

'You managed?'

'Let's just go.'

It was seven fifty am, and the traffic was heavy. I cursed the Icelanders and their habit of leaving late for work. We were only two kilometres away from the hospital, but at this rate we'd be having the baby in the cab. Another contraction began.

'Shouldn't you call an ambulance?' asked the driver.

Olanda was crying. How did you call an ambulance from a taxi, anyway? The traffic eased as we came into the hospital. The driver pulled up at the door, wished us good luck, and pressed the doorbell. As we entered the lift, Olanda collapsed on my shoulder. I swivelled her into the maternity ward. A pair of midwives greeted us with barely disguised horror. They reached for a wheelchair.

'Straight to the delivery room, I think,' said one.

'Yes, quite,' said the other.

They were lovely, and spoke good English. One, Guðrún, who would do the bulk of the coaxing and coaching, wore glasses and smiled with gushing, gummy goodwill. The other, Berglind, was more experienced and played a more considered role. She hovered and checked, and made jokes.

'You'll get to meet him in a moment,' she said. 'Isn't that exciting?'

'Yes,' said Olanda. 'Yes.'

'Let's see how everything's going down there,' added Guðrún. She measured Olanda. 'Goodness. You've dilated seven centimetres already.'

'Is that good? What does that mean?' asked Olanda.

'It means, sweetheart, that you've done most of the work on your own,' replied Berglind. 'You're nearly there.'

It was eight thirty am. I put on a CD of Mozart and looked outside. It was raining lightly, again. We were on the ocean side of the hospital and out to sea I could see thick clouds still gathered from the night before. The road beneath us was quieter now. Everyone was at work.

Inside, there began rounds of encouragement. She was getting there; she was doing so well; she was such a brave girl; she would get to meet her little boy soon; look, he was starting to show a little bit. All these from Guðrún and Berglind. My job was a different one. It had been given to me by our instructor, my one thing, and I wasn't going to let Olanda down now.

'Breathe,' I said. 'Remember to breathe.'

'I am,' she replied. She screamed.

'There,' said Guðrún. 'You're so close.'

'Breathe,' I said. 'Just breathe.'

'Stop telling me to breathe!'

And, then, in one of those moments that you thought you had brought yourself to expect, he was with us, our son Finnur Kári, born at nine thirty-seven am on 5 July 2006. Into a stainless world, it must be said.

I laughed. And a moment later I was sobbing and laughing at the same time.

And then I remembered to breathe.

Finnur's birth, from the first contraction to his appearance in the world of midwives, hospital blankets, scales and measuring tape, had taken just over six hours. It was only midmorning. How, I wondered, did anyone have a child by midmorning?

Guðrún and Berglind said they would leave us to ourselves, but would be back in an hour or so to move us to our room.

'Are you alright, darling?' asked Olanda.

'Yes, yes, of course. I'm fine.'

We looked at each other. And then we looked at Finnur. There was no escaping it: we were parents. I sent a dozen text messages to our friends and family in Australia, and to my relations in Reykjavík.

'He's very quiet,' I said.

'Asleep even,' replied Olanda.

'You look as though you need some sleep, too.'

'Yes. And you must be hungry.'

'Not too bad,' I said. 'But I do have an important task.'

'Really?'

'It won't take long,' I answered. Well, I hoped it wouldn't. When we had become engaged, I had offered Olanda a poem. I thought it was time I bought a ring.

'I really feel like a hamburger,' I said.

'Go and get a hamburger, then.' I asked her to stand by the window.

'When you see me, wave. Then get some sleep.'

I ran down the stairs to Miklabraut and waved. I had taken my photo of the window at which she stood holding Finnur, or at which I hoped she still stood. It was too shadowy to tell. I walked back around to the other, sunny side of the building and on to Laugavegur, and to a Swiss jeweller.

In a couple of months, I was going to be thirty-four. It would be seventeen years since, as a seventeen year old, I had met my father at the car yard and gone with him for a drive to the president's lodge. He had asked me to keep his paternity a secret, and in the hope that it would bring us closer I had agreed. As often as I have told myself that I was past caring about him—which, for the most part, I was—even now I couldn't suppress the wish that he would contact me. He didn't. But he did ask my brother, Björn, to pass on his congratulations.

Gísli and I would remain apart, each on our own side of a rift that ran through Thingvellir and divided the country, its families, and all the disputes that over the centuries would be recorded and then forgotten. I had tried to reach across the divide, and in doing so I had become a father. That was a good result, a homecoming.

Gísli and I had been joined in a strange sort of conspiracy: to complicate the lives of the women we loved. Iceland was to blame, of course—before you knew it, you were not only trying to live there yourself, but involving the innocent, too. But I wasn't really up to it; I couldn't push that hard for Iceland. We would return to Brisbane in time for Christmas. And maybe one day we would return again. And maybe Finnur would want to live there. And so on.

It was late July. I hadn't done much since Finnur's birth—it was all sleepless nights and late walks; the pram was Finnur's preferred mode of getting to sleep. Greg, the athlete in our group of friends in Brisbane, came to visit. He looked at me, and sighed. What I needed was a good walk and a long swim.

'Where do you want to walk?' I asked.

'Esja, of course,' he said.

'A mountain, then.'

'Yes. Let's take on Esja. You're always saying how much you love it.'

We set off on a bright, warm morning. A sign in the car park said, 'Be careful on the track. Take your time. The return walk to the top is about eight hours.'

'Six, surely,' replied Greg to the sign.

To begin with, the going was easy. Sheep track walking, really. Then for an hour or so we hit scree, and the temperature rose. Another walker said something about it being the warmest day ever recorded in Reykjavík.

'What would that mean?' asked Greg.

'Probably that it's hit twenty.'

For a few minutes, Greg stopped running. We were into the last section, an exposed zigzag of narrow paths, the final cliff face, and the part of Esja that on winter days made such a difference to the view of the bay.

'Three hours to the top,' said Greg, when we neared the summit. 'Back down in two and a half.'

'Food, first,' I replied. Greg looked handsomely towards Reykjavík. 'You haven't even broken a sweat,' I went on. 'Aren't you jet-lagged?'

'How could you be jet-lagged here?'

It was Reykjavík, but as I'd never seen it before, as flat and exposed to the sea as a slip of blond beachfront in Australia.

'I've always wanted to have a swim in the midnight sun,' said Greg as we began our descent.

'Well, the pool's open till ten,' I replied. 'Not midnight, but close.'

'Not the pool, though.'

'It's pretty cold in the sea,' I joked.

'Really? Not that bad, surely.'

He did want to swim in the sea. So that evening we rode to an artificial beach that had been built at Nauthólsvík, a small bay at the side of the airport. Even it had a warmed-up section, with hoses pumping hot spring water down to the shallows. No, said Greg, it had to be the open sea.

'You're getting in, too, by the way,' he continued.

It was cold. I was tired. But he had me, because it was light at midnight, allowing the odd Fokker 50 to still come in from the south, and because pale, orange light lit the water.

'Just get in,' called Greg.

Across the fjord lay Álftanes, lying on its side like a tired old man. And the road to the president's lodge. I had never been back. An invitation once came from the university, but even then I'd shied away from the chance. I was glad I hadn't returned. A short swim in that direction was enough.

REYKJAVÍK, 2010

In July 2010 I made another of my now yearly visits to Iceland—my research still takes me there on a regular basis. Olanda and I have been living in Brisbane for over four years, since the Christmas after Finnur's birth, and we now have a second son, Magnús, who was born in Brisbane two years ago.

My mother looks after the boys two days a week, but when I am travelling she helps out a little more than that. On my return she naturally fills me in on what they've been doing, and the little things they've said. I once replied to the updates by asking whether Finnur wasn't a bit of a handful—he likes to have adult company all of the time.

'Don't be so sure,' she answered. 'You were much worse. If I was on the phone, you'd throw your shoes at me. You couldn't stand it if I talked to anyone else.'

When I left for Iceland this last July, I promised to bring him home some ash from the eruption at Eyjafjallajökull—all Finnur and I had talked about for weeks was the volcano, how volcanoes were formed, and the different kinds of lava formations they produced. I said I'd drive to the volcano, which happens to be located in the heart of *Njál's Saga* country, and collect it myself.

'You won't go too close, will you?' he asked.

'No, no, just to the edge of the ash. I'll be safe, I'm sure.'

I had another reason for visiting this time. My sister Fríða was getting married, and she'd asked me to play a song at the service. I wondered openly how Ólöf would feel, having me there in the centre of things; Fríða wasn't sure, either. Ólöf knew I was a presence in my siblings' lives, but she still didn't like to talk about me. But maybe this was the time for reconciliation, and a fresh start.

The wedding was held late on a clear, warm afternoon. I arrived early with Halldór, with whom I still write and play music, to set up and do a sound check. Soon after we'd finished getting ready, my brother Björn arrived, and then Ólöf with my sisters Anna and Bryndís. Following them were streams of Finnur and Magnús' cousins, each with a role in the service, and each dressed in light, summer formal wear.

It was the first time I'd seen Ólöf since 1999, when I contacted my siblings, and the nervousness of those days rushed back to me. Perhaps it was the same for her, because she responded in exactly the same way as she did during that first family dinner, drawing me to her and welcoming me.

Gísli was too ill to attend the service, and I suspect that helped the rest of us to relax. He had faded from my life, that is, no longer an absence that I took much notice of. And he was now less of a responsibility for Ólöf, too: the advance of Parkinson's disease meant that he was in permanent hospital care these days, with little chance of ever returning to his own place.

After the wedding service, I was pulled to the Ólafs family table and told once again a fact that I'd heard from a number of sources, including my mother, that Ólöf was a gifted singer and had more or less given up her music for Gísli and the family. I asked whether she and my sisters would sing for the table.

'No, not now,' she replied, smiling. 'I don't sing as often these days.'

'What song would you like to hear?' asked Bryndís from across the other side of the table.

'There is a folk song I love, although I only really know it from Ragnheiður Gröndal's version. It's called "Sofðu unga ástín mín". I'm sure you both know it well.'

Bryndís began singing and, despite her hesitation, after the first few bars Ólöf joined her.

Sofðu, unga ástín mín,	Sleep, my darling child,
—úti regnið grætur.	—outside the rain weeps.
Mamma geymir gullin þín,	Mother will keep your treasures safe,
gamla leggi og völuskrín.	your old bone and the toy box.
Við skulum ekki vaka um dimmar nætur.	We won't wake in the dark night.
Það er margt sem myrkrið veit,	There is so much the darkness knows,
—minn er hugur þungur.	—mine are heavy thoughts.

Oft ég svarta sandinn leit	Often I saw the black sand
svíða grænan engireit.	scorch the green earth.
Í jöklinum hljóða	The glacier's dead-deep
dauðadjúpar sprungur.	cracks call.
Sofðu lengi, sofðu rótt,	Sleep long, sleep peacefully,
—seint mun bezt að vakna.	—it is best to wake late.
Mæðan kenna mun þér	Sorrow will soon teach you,
fljótt,	
meðan hallar degi skjótt,	while the day quickly fades,
að mennirnir elska, missa,	that men love, lose, cry, and
gráta og sakna.	grieve.

Egil the warrior–poet had long ago sung a poem for his lost son, a song of love, loss, and grief. Still today, when we sing for our children, mostly we reveal ourselves.

***

I was again staying with Bergur and Rut, and got back to their place at three in the morning. It had been a long and happy party of dancing and drinking, and I slept only fitfully until nine, when the thought of driving to the volcano overcame my ability to lay still. There is no need to set out early in summer—it's light all day. But I feared that if I left it too late I'd give up on the search and, instead, do as my friends had suggested, and buy bottled ash from the airport souvenir shop.

Around noon I crossed the heath of lava, volcanoes and hot springs that lies between Reykjavík and Hveragerði, and shortly afterwards at the small agricultural town of Selfoss I stopped for a hot dog and chocolate milk; not exactly a hangover cure but a boost for the second hour of the drive.

At the village of Hvolsvöllur I couldn't resist taking the inland road, which would allow me to approach the volcano along Fljótshlíð, the district of Gunnar of Hlíðarendi that I had last visited in 1999 with Bergur and Rut and the Canadian family. The road wound to the northern side of Markarfljót. There were wide pastures on my right, while the *hlíð* or 'slope' on my left rose in irregular steps of home meadows and sheltering woods. The wind was picking up as the day wore on and occasionally I felt the car pushed towards the estuary that traced through the flat expanse of river debris to the south.

I took the car up to the old church at Hlíðarendi, following a crumbling driveway that was attended by half a dozen horses that approached the car for a treat that I couldn't offer—I had eaten all my doughnuts. I still hadn't found any volcanic ash, but from the church I saw that it was about to find me. A vast cloud of the stuff was approaching from Thórsmörk, the deep valley to the east. Beneath me a line of fifty horses, led by half a dozen riders, was escaping its advance, and presented a rich, nomadic image: the south of Iceland was transformed into the site of a desert storm.

Back on the road, visibility was reduced to about thirty metres, and I began to think better of my promise of ash. A headache from the night before had been shadowing me for the past hour, and with the ash thick in the air I suddenly found the drive a strain. I pushed on to Seljalandsfoss, a waterfall at the base of Eyjafjallajökull, and then, still unable to find ash on the ground, gave up and returned to Reykjavík empty-handed.

The next day I flew to London, and in the evening on to Brisbane, where Finnur was waiting impatiently for his delivery. I had had no choice. After checking in at Keflavík, I had rushed to the airport souvenir shop and bought a sample of navy-grey sparkles presented in what must have been intended as a test tube. It was certified, by a small sticker with bold type, as coming from the 2010 eruption. Had it been possible, I would have extracted more from my lungs.

ASHES

A sample of Icelandic ash sits in pride of place on Finnur's bookshelf. More than once it's been carefully packed into the side pocket of his red backpack to take to kindergarten for show and tell. He is becoming quite the expert about Iceland. Although, he resists the language. The best I have managed is to read his Icelandic books in the original and then translate them straight away into English. Never just Icelandic, he tells me strictly.

During Fríða's wedding, I resisted urges from my sisters to visit Gísli. They were looking for a reconciliation—they thought it would be the last chance for father and son to find each other before his illness became worse still. I didn't make it, not least because I didn't think he'd want it himself. I assured my sisters that I wouldn't regret it later, it was too late for regrets of that kind, and it was best to let things lie. He died on 8 September 2010.

My immediate physical reaction to the news was a pit of regret that formed in my stomach, and told me that I'd made the wrong decision not to see him. I knew now that I had never entirely given up on him. What I had managed was to feel all right without him, and to realise that Iceland existed without his presence in my life. I had not managed to stop loving him, and I know well enough that if you can you should say good-bye to the ones you love. Fríða knew it, too.

For Christmas, she and my other siblings gave me Gísli's watch, and I find myself wearing it with as much pride as Finnur shows when he takes his volcanic ash to show his class-mates. A tube of silver ash and a Swiss watch: they seem to me emblems of both continuity and change, how time passes but inevitably brings with it much of the past. I like that relation-ship between the past and the present very much. We are all capable of being bridges across the decades, rifts in the land-scape, hemispheres even.

Twenty years ago, I had wanted my father to sign a docu-ment stating his paternity. It was, I thought, my way back to Iceland. Now, after his death, Fríða discovered at the magis-trate's office that they needed my signature. By some silent miracle of Icelandic record keeping, I had come to be listed as one of Gísli's children. I was asked to join the others in signing off on his estate.

I was shocked, and asked Fríða to go back and check: I had never corrected the Icelandic records, and couldn't understand how I'd suddenly appeared as one of his children. Fríða came back with the same news: it was all quite official. I was his son.

I signed my part of the form. In doing so, I suppose I was providing the signature for a form I'd long wanted Gísli to sign—I officiated over my own entry into the record books. I was bridging another of the rifts that ran in often unpredictable directions from Gísli's request for secrecy to my life as a father. Next time I'm in Iceland, I'll check to see whether my birth certificate has also been quietly amended.

Gísli had been ill for many years: the early stages of Parkinson's had been present during the family lunch at Hveragerði just over ten years before, and I'd told Mum then that he was much changed. The first images she'd seen of him as an unwell middle-aged man had upset her. News of his death struck her with the mixed and conflicted emotions of the years that they had together, and the enterprise of parenting that they had for the most part undertaken thousands of miles apart. She was sad about him, but perhaps in the way that she had always been sad about him. She loved him, and she felt his loss, but he hadn't ever quite been there, either.

Lovers slip away into the water; they usually take something of us with them. In January 2011, we heard that Ed was ill, and a few days later, before we'd had time to see him, he had died. I drove Mum to the funeral, held just a couple of hours' to the south of Ocean Shores, talking a little about Ed as we went. We rehearsed their life together, their rambling adventures of the 1960s, and their separation.

'He has died the same age as Gísli,' said Mum.

'And just months apart,' I added, 'the two men in your life.'

I didn't ask her, as Bolli had once asked his mother Guðrún, whom she loved most, but I couldn't quite suppress the thought, either. I have written a book that claims to know that my mother loved Gísli, but as we drove through the roadworks at the Gold Coast, I wondered if Ed hadn't been the one all along, her first love and the one who had in a sense led her to Gísli.

She changed their lives beyond measure. Gísli, I had been told, had only ever loved two women, his wife and my mother. And after the funeral, Ed's son Beau told me that in a memoir that Ed had been composing, he'd written that Mum was the love of his life. He'd never gotten over her.

I told Mum.

'Why didn't he ever say as much?' she asked.

Perhaps theirs was not the generation to make declarations of that kind too easily. And hadn't Ed, Mum, and Gísli always been rather good at keeping things to themselves?

I have taken a different approach, and for some time have looked back on the stories about Mum, Ed, and Gísli with a view to getting them down on paper: I suppose my generation tends to declare its feelings more openly, and I am by nature the type who writes things out in order to understand them. I must admit that I wonder how my story will be interpreted by my own children, when they eventually come to join in the creation of the past with their own reading of this book.

The promises of Iceland have, over the years, changed. I've told the boys that we'll all go to Iceland next year, and of course I would like it if Finnur and Magnús felt something of the connection that I do. Who knows, one day they may find they have another home there. For home, I have discovered, is not a moment in the past to which one returns, or a revision. It isn't even the feeling of being settled in the place you love most. At the end of this story, my overwhelming feeling is that home is the knowledge that one day you will be back. That, I suppose, is what I have been doing all along: going back to Iceland. And going back to Australia, too. Promises are so often two-sided.

ACKNOWLEDGEMENTS

I hope this book reveals the enormous personal debt I owe to many of the people it features. The relationship with Iceland that it represents would not have been possible without the generous support and love of Bergur and Rut and their children Kári, Kolbrún and Rakel; my siblings Fríða, Anna, Bryndís and Björn; and my mother Susan. To Olanda and the boys, saying thank you seems inadequate, so for you I add a *takk* instead.

I am also very grateful to friends and colleagues who commented on earlier drafts of this book, in particular Anne Collins, Stuart Glover, Stefanie Gropper, Sarah Holland-Batt, Sam Martin and Anthony May. Our conversations have not only helped me to shape the story, but also to better understand my role in it. I also thank Madonna Duffy, Joanne Holliman and John Hunter at UQP, who edited my book with great care and sensitivity.